*Wonder, the Rainbow, and the
Aesthetics of Rare Experiences*

Wonder, the Rainbow, and the Aesthetics of Rare Experiences

PHILIP FISHER

Harvard University Press

Cambridge, Massachusetts, and London, England   1998

Library of Congress Cataloging-in-Publication Data

Fisher, Philip.
Wonder, the rainbow, and the aesthetics of rare experiences /
Philip Fisher.
   p.   cm.
Includes bibliographical references and index.
ISBN 0-674-95561-7 (cloth : alk. paper)

1. Wonder (Philosophy) 2. Aesthetics. I. Title.
BH301.W65   1998
111′.85—dc21   98-22515

Designed by Gwen Nefsky Frankfeldt

Contents

Contents

*Wonder, the Rainbow, and the
Aesthetics of Rare Experiences*

The Aesthetics of Rare Experiences

Wonder and the Sublime

The experience of wonder no less than that of the sublime makes up part of the aesthetics of rare experiences. Each depends on moments in which we find ourselves struck by effects within nature whose power over us depends on their not being common or everyday. Both wonder and the sublime are also categories within the aesthetics of surprise and the sudden, as is that favorite modern aesthetic category, shock. Finally, they are both experiences tied to the visual taken in a deeply intellectual way; they both lead us back to reflection on ourselves and on our human powers; and they both have deep connections to mathematics, as Kant showed in the case of what he called the mathematical sublime, and to whatever link there might be between mathematics and the most essential details of thinking itself. How we think and how we are drawn to think about just this, rather than just that, will be the subject of this book.

Modern thought since Romanticism and the philosophy of Kant and Burke has been more interested in the sublime than in wonder. In part this is because aesthetic experience has been exploited, in T. E. Hulme's phrase, as a form of spilt religion within romanticism.[1] In Hulme's metaphor, the emotions inspired in us by God, eternity, and the universe as a whole and held within the jar of religion—feelings of the infinite, adoration, fear, the sublime—spill out in the process of secularization onto such parts of experience as our relation to landscape, the nearly religious importance of romantic love, and our worshipful interest in our own subjectivity.

The sublime secularized religious feelings of the infinite and of the relative insignificance of human powers in an attractive way, allowing the modern intellectual to hold onto covert religious feelings under an aesthetic disguise. Romanticism, along with the neo-Catholicism of decadence, the Wagnerian rebirth of myth, Symbolism, and even modernism itself had this component of carrying on, behind the back of the secular enlightenment, religious practices in the catacombs of the aesthetic, a technique pioneered within the aesthetics of the sublime. At the same time, in an industrial civilization more and more enchanted with the growth of human power over nature, the sublime was a covert antitechnological rebuke, an intellectual rearguard action against the steam engine of James Watt that would change the ratio of human power to natural forces forever.

In the sublime, fear and surprise, power and danger occur in a rich blend. The sublime could be called the aestheticization of fear. Wonder, the most neglected of primary aesthetic experiences within modernity, involves the aestheticization of delight, or of the pleasure principle rather than the death principle, whose agent within aesthetic experience is the sublime. The aesthetic sublime led so quickly to bombastic forms of music and, especially, painting that, with the exception of Wagner and Géricault, philosophical interest in the sublime has carried on happily a hundred years after the effect itself was aesthetically extinct and in a period where even the greatest landscape painting, that of Cézanne and Monet, has had little to do with this experience. With only a few exceptions, the sublime was an aesthetic category more important in the realm of kitsch than in high art. For that reason, as an aesthetic effect, the sublime should not be thought of as the alternative to the beautiful. It has more in common with such effects as the noble, the pious, or the grotesque, that area of aesthetics where we most often find second-rate artists compensating by invoking either strong effects or right thinking.

With the sublime we have for two hundred years built up a more and more intricate theory for a type of art that we do not actually have and would not care for if we did have it. Once we look at the visual arts, especially architecture and painting since 1873, the founding moment of Impressionism, we have to be struck by the signs of a pervasive appeal to the experience of wonder. In architecture this is true in part because of the many new materials and building techniques that made possible, in combination, the construction of things never before seen on the earth. The most obvious example is the skyscraper, the first genuinely vertical building type in history, set in relation to the sky rather than the earth, surrendering at last the heavy mass, broadest in its base, that was the very essence of a building up to that moment. After the skyscraper it became possible to see just how much every previous building had been an exploration of the horizontal with only towers and lighthouses as exceptions. With skyscrapers we find ourselves in a new aesthetics of the city, forged out of the combination of electric lighting and the glass and metal of thin geometric forms rising straight up to heights previously of no use to humans. These new forms came clad in surfaces of glass, steel, or aluminum, the new materials of our century, arranged in sheets of repeating rectangles. Alongside the spatial thrill of these chaste forms, we also find in modern architecture and modern engineering striking cantilevered effects, in fact beams without posts, a second surprise equal to that earlier wonder, the arch.

Skyscrapers are our modern pyramids but without the look and heavy geometry of a cone of poured sand, bottom heavy, that pyramids have. The skyscraper has the apparent weightlessness of a single metal rod without a base, or with no visible base, since it has been driven with pile drivers into the bedrock below the ground and uses the inner earth itself as its concealed base. The modern skyscraper depends on the great steel mills of the late nineteenth century, most of which produced rails for the tens of thousands of miles of railroad track being laid across America and Europe. Once redundant lines crisscrossed the earth, the output of steel began to be shifted into the vertical dimension, and rails were laid up into the sky in a frame construction around which the skyscraper's outer shell could be wrapped.

Architecture, in the years following modern steel and plate glass manufacturing, stands within an aesthetics of wonder because the long history of buildings made of wood, stone, grass, brick, bamboo, mud, and even marble provided no clues to what might work or take place next with the use of these new materials and within the new engineering of stresses and loads that was now possible. The architecture and the engineering of our time set us face to face with a radical newness within materials, within the organization of forces, and within spatial possibilities of a breath-taking kind, like that of working in an office on the fortieth floor or walking along a street lined with varied spikelike buildings more than a hundred times our own height. Architects in the last hundred years have addressed or solicited an aesthetic response of delight, a feeling of seeing the impossible happen, as we feel with the George Washington Bridge or the buildings of Chicago. Architecture set out to produce experiences of wonder.

On a smaller scale, the modern house from Frank Lloyd Wright or Le Corbusier to Richard Meier, Frank Gehry, or Peter Eisenman has orchestrated a similar pleasure of radical surprise, a novelty of material and effect that is the counterpart to the more obvious novelty of the business and urban architecture of our time. The materials as well as the size in which building was now possible with reinforced concrete, steel beam structure, and lightweight outer surfaces set up the physical premise for an aesthetics of wonder.

As we can see from certain architectural drawings of the early twentieth century, a number of Expressionist architects toyed with the idea of using the same materials and urban scale for a sinister, shadowy, intimidating architecture of fear. When we see these drawings it becomes clear that the modern architecture that was actually built was an architecture of light, of sun and blue skies, a radiant city as Le Corbusier liked to call it, a city built partly in response to the smoke-blackened stone of the nineteenth-century city. Fortunately, it was the modern corporation with its optimism and confidence, its pleasure in power and in pleasure itself, that ordered and paid for these buildings, leaving unbuilt the brooding, shadow-crossed, sinister buildings of German Expressionist architecture, now visible only in the films of the 1920s, where their nightmarish shadows repeat the sinister Victorian city without regard for the entirely new urban world that had been created.

The material newness in architecture ran parallel to a century of painting in which, after Monet's first Impressionist work of 1873, a restless invention of new and unprecedented ways of painting indicated the search for a similar impact of complete technical freshness, as though some completely unprecedented thing were now going on at the spot where painting used to take place. The century that saw the choppy, bright strokes of Monet, the system of Cézanne, the flat bright colors of Matisse and Gauguin, the Cubist surface invented by Picasso and Braque, the dripped stringlike paintings of Pollock, the color field paintings of the American 1960s or the systematic work of Mondrian, has been defined by the technical search of many painters for an unprecedented look, a striking freshness, as though a whole new genre were in front of us and not simply more paintings of this or that kind—landscapes or portraits, allegorical history paintings or still-lifes.

The appeal of these works is not to an aesthetics of shock. Shock flourishes within the arts of time and particularly within such temporal problems as those of boredom and habit. Shock is a rejuvenation within fatigued systems of representation and thought. That is why the classical and religious mind of Baudelaire gave us our greatest poet of the aesthetics of shock. With shock we face the all or nothing, the Russian roulette of a mind or a system at the end of its rope. It is a last rather than a first move within experience. Surrealism, that most fatigued of modern art movements, is our own debilitated gambler with shock, squeezing some last life out of fatigued symbols by juxtaposing bizarre combinations among them—the melting watch, the banal combinations of Magritte, and those of the very appropriately named Max Ernst.

From Monet to Pollock, technical newness in painting has been tied to energy that could be demonstrated on the surface of the work, and to an excitement that is sometimes hectic and sometimes the sensual glow of ripe attention, as in the late paintings of Monet. The address to the viewer of these great and often oversized works of the last century has been an address to the aesthetics of wonder; that is, to the feeling of radical singularity of means and purposes, to the idea of incomparable experiences, to the self-consciously fresh or first work in a technical direction where preparation for seeing it breaks down and gives few clues. But with wonder, above all else, there is the address to delight, to the bold youthful stroke, to pleasure in the unexpected and in the extension of means outside the limits where they might be thought to come to an end. The rapid wearing out of the new is also part of the aesthetics of wonder. The right timing of abandonment is as crucial as the moment of surprising entry. The very powerful, brooding, but very tired Cubist paintings that Braque carried on to the end of his life are part of the pathos of aging within an aesthetic of the quick and the fresh.

The narrative arts, for reasons that will be made clear later, have fewer chances within the aesthetics of wonder, although the nearly spatial poetry that follows Mallarmé and leads on to Rilke and Celan aims for the pleasures of a radical novelty and exoticism of sensation, and even of a rarity within combinations of words, that are signs of the appeal to wonder. Where painting and architecture find ever new continents of technique and materials to explore, language remains the only given material of poetry and narration. As a result the very basis for architectural wonder that rests on the effects of our first experiences of never before used materials is denied to writing.

An aesthetics of wonder is required by the art that we already find ourselves living within. That such an aesthetics has its alternative in the aesthetics of fear will be one of the claims of the pages that follow. That an aesthetics of wonder has to do with a border between sensation and thought, between aesthetics and science is another claim of my argument. That memory and narrative are antagonistic to an aesthetics of wonder will be one of the unexpected aesthetic discoveries of the pages that follow.

One core result of the argument that follows will be that there is a lively border between an aesthetics of wonder and what we might call a poetics of thought. How we think and what it is that leads us to think about this rather than that are topics within the aesthetics of wonder. The details of thought, of problem solving, of the analysis of works of art where a slow unfolding of attention and questioning takes place in the presence of the work are all questions within the domain of wonder.

The argument that follows will work along the path that runs at the border between an aesthetics of wonder and a poetics of thought. It will be equally engaged with examples from philosophy, science, mathematics, and art. Each of my key illustrations, diverse as they may seem, will unfold the surprise of intelligibility, that moment when the puzzling snaps into sharp focus and is grasped with pleasure.

After a first characterization of the conditions of wonder, I will use three cases that might, at first, seem far afield from one another. These are:

First. The history of the curiosity about and the progressive explanation of the rainbow. How did the combination of pleasure and puzzlement in the face of rainbows lead to a scientific explanation? As a further question, did that explanation drain the aesthetic pleasure that had drawn us to think about rainbows in the first place? How did the rainbow become intelligible under the allure of wonder? Did it, once explained, force us to trade off knowledge for pleasure, intelligibility for wonder?

Second. A simple and very famous example from philosophy and mathematics, the challenge to double the area of a given square. How do the phases of bafflement, trial and error, and final surprise of what we call "getting it" display the experience of wonder in simple problem solving? How do the baffling details snap into place and yield the feeling of intelligibility?

Third. As we find ourselves drawn by the expectation of pleasure and the force of curiosity in front of a work of art, a contemporary painting of a kind that we have never seen before and whose details and content seem unintelligible to us, what path of thought leads us to the feeling of familiarity that is aligned to what we call "getting it" in the experience of solving problems?

My motive in using examples drawn from mathematics (the doubled square), from the science of everyday experiences (the rainbow), and from painting (a contemporary, abstract work of art) is to look behind or through the very distinct procedures within each of these domains to a common poetics of wonder, a map of the features of thinking that guide us to satisfaction and a feeling of intelligibility within experience. The local feeling of intelligibility is what we call, in simple cases like a joke or a reference, the feeling of "getting it." The state we linger in before this moment of "getting it" lasts sometimes for a few seconds and sometimes for months, and in this state we say "I just don't get it!" The path from the puzzling to the feeling of intelligibility raises, among other questions, the issue of just why certain things puzzle us. Not everything that we do not know or cannot ever know puzzles us and draws us into thinking about it in an attempt to explain it to our own satisfaction. At the other end of this path, the satisfaction of intelligibility, or what I call "local intelligibility," is different from what a philosopher would call knowing and it is even more remote from what Descartes called certain knowledge.

The feeling of intelligibility is like an ocean surrounding the small island of things that we truly know. Every century and every culture lives in a world that it finds intelligible even though other times and cultures believe that errors, false hypotheses, and a basic lack of the tools of later intelligibility left earlier and other cultures with a texture of intelligibility riddled with flaws. At the outer borders of what we think about and have some idea of, we go on thinking even though many of the tools we use are wrong or inadequate when viewed from later perspectives that will, in their turn, seem to be flawed and inadequate when viewed by still later perspectives. How do thinking and the satisfaction of local intelligibility go on while unsuspected deep flaws are carried forward within thinking? It is in this broad sea of intelligibility that so often turns out to need later and still later revision that the clear link between what we do in looking at a work of art and what we do in solving a problem or explaining an object of everyday experience like a rainbow can be found. In all three cases we are engaged in an ongoing fragile project of making sense, and it is the nature of making sense rather than the nature of knowing that is my concern.

Descartes wanted to wipe the slate clean so as to start from the few clear and distinct ideas that we might be certain that we know. New truths might be added only if they too were certain and clear. In everyday life we cannot think only by means of or about those things of which we are certain. Every culture must have a medical science no matter how thin or error-ridden its truths. Disease and death are made intelligible within every flawed and partial medical system because we confront illness not when we are ready and equipped with certain ideas but when it strikes. Under the rules of time, bad ideas are better than none at all because a dark requirement for any action at all is the background feeling of the world's intelligibility.

There is no more interesting question than how we carry out the antiphilosophical project of working with and improving the mixed web of error, uncertainty, the unknown and the unknowable while thinking and reaching results. Socrates insisted that to know what it is that we do not know is the humbling first step of true knowledge. We need to add that the impossibility of knowing any such thing is one of the things that strikes us when we look closely at the reasoning and science of the past, even in the moments of its greatest accomplishments, seventeenth-century physics or nineteenth- and twentieth-century medicine. When we look at the history of successful explanation and ask how it could be that it remained undamaged by the unreliable tools, unavailable technology, hidden errors carried on through the entire project of thought, inadequate basic terminology, sectors of ignorance built in like blank spots on a map and sometimes taking up 90 percent of the map itself, then we can see just how fruitful the idea of local intelligibility is as the necessary alternative to certain knowledge. Defective but still manageable rationality is what we actually have to use to make sense of the objects of our curiosity.

Wonder drives and sustains the defective rationality that gives us intelligibility under conditions where we will not even know that we have reached certain knowledge when and if we have.

Philosophy Begins in Wonder

Fear made the gods, but philosophy begins in wonder. By splicing these two sayings together we graft the contrast between religion and philosophy onto the history of the passions. Religion and mythology, in the saying "Fear made the gods," depend on an explanation of the world in terms of an experience which begins in fear and then leads on to phases of propitiation and punishment until ending in sacrifice or atonement, those two profoundly religious forms of apology. The world of fear is one in which we are constantly in danger and constantly in the wrong. A world made reasonable by fear is inevitably a world of sin and punishment because part of the reasonableness of this world is the belief that we have deserved whatever it is that we now fear.

On the horizon of this world made intelligible by fear is the reminder of just how much more horrible the perceived alternative explanation must have been for this one to be so acceptable that it has been the most stable, rational account of nature and experience for most times and most people. The position of Adam and, one generation later, Cain, called by name after just having done wrong, and about to be punished with what we know to be everyday human existence itself, work and wandering, this position of the burden and threat of the ordinary and the everyday, a world in which Cain's fate of never being able to die is an even more horrible punishment than Adam's of being, now for the first time, condemned to die, this is the sketch of the starting point, the genealogy of human experience seen through one version of the aperture of the passion of fear. Fear and the gods yield an intelligible world.

An equally intelligible world unfolds from the claim that philosophy begins in wonder. It is in the Platonic dialogue *Theaetetus* that Socrates connected philosophy to wonder in the words that became the famous phrase. Socrates spoke in response to the words of Theaetetus, who had reached a point of total confusion and described himself as "lost in wonder when I think of all these things."[2]

Wonder is, in this case, the famous Socratic moment of knowing one's ignorance, knowing that one does not know. As Theaetetus said in expanding his words, "it really makes my head swim." Socrates passes over the word "lost" in Theaetetus' description to say that this "feeling of wonder shows that you are a philosopher, since wonder is the only beginning of philosophy, and he who said that Iris was the child of Thaumas made a good genealogy."[3] The feeling *(pathos)* of wonder *(to thaumalein)* is, in Plato's Greek, the only *arche philoso-phias,* with the word *arche* used as in our word Archeology, the study of the earliest state of things. Naturally the word *arche* leaves open the question whether wonder exists only before philosophy, defining pre-philosophy, a source whose disappearance marks the beginning of real philosophy, or whether it continues to be the passionate moment that brings on thought in every occasion of philosophy. Philosophy itself here is understood in the widest sense of knowledge, science, wisdom. It would include geometry, astronomy, the study of ethics, aesthetics, politics, the law, and so on.

In English, the word "wonder" is used in two senses. The first is that of interrogation, where wonder is a verb ("I wonder why . . ."). The sum of the many questions, "I wonder why . . .?" makes up the activity of science, in so far as science is the power to notice and put in question, rather than the power to answer. The second use is in exclamation, where "wonder" is a noun ("What a wonder!"). English preserves the connection between intellectual curiosity ("I wonder if . . .) and the pleasure of amazement, that is, wonder taken in the aesthetic sense of admiration, delight in the qualities of a thing. Admiration in its root *mira* is, of course, the Latin word for wonder and also the root word for miracle.

After his remarkable compliment to philosophy in the first half of his sentence, why does Socrates then go on to speak of the goddess Iris and her father, Thaumas? Thaumatology will remain until the Renaissance in Europe the term for the science of wonders and for miracles, that theological form of wonder that must in the end be excluded from the meaning of wonder if a modern concept of science is to be set in place. Thaumas is the god identified here by Socrates as the etymology of the word *thaumalein* (wonders).

Iris, his daughter, is the rainbow. That the rainbow is the "daughter" of wonder makes it far more than one wonder among many. It is, we might say, the first and central instance, bound to wonder not just as one item in a list, but by ties of family, as the only known child. To understand philosophy we must go to its *arche* wonder, but to think out wonder we must descend genetically (father to daughter) to the rainbow. Philosophy and the rainbow appear across the fulcrum of wonder, by which they are both to be known, and are understood to be related in the most fundamental way: the way of *arche* and *genealogein.*

Iris is, in Hesiod's *Theogony,* the messenger of the gods, just as heaven is the face of the gods or just as Apollo is both the sun itself and the god of light. What we think of scientifically as the objects of nature (sun, thunder, light, rainbow) are not here separated from three things: first, from the form of existence that we call personality (each thing is given identity and personal history); second, from agency (no force is understood without an agent whose force it is and whose decision to use that force is understood); and, finally, from worship, fear, gratitude, and pleasure—no object of nature is cut off from our response to it, from our delight or fear in its presence.

The name Iris imposes all three of these conditions on the rainbow. The term Iris would continue to be used in all scientific works on the rainbow down to the time of Newton—so long as they were written in Latin or translated from the Greek or Arabic into Latin. The most common Latin title for a scientific work on the rainbow, *De Iride,* carries on the presence of this goddess within the most advanced scientific work on light, color, and the rainbow from Aristotle through Ptolemy, Grosseteste, Bacon, Theodoric of Freiberg, Descartes, and Newton. Only Descartes, publishing in French, deliberately avoided the mythological and poetic, but nonetheless everyday French word Iris. He wrote of *l'arc-en-ciel* so as to insist on the ordinary. Even the English word rainbow, or rain-bow, while seeming prosaic, uses the word "bow" to describe the semicircular form, and in doing this we repoeticize the term with an analogy to a bow and arrow even while insisting, with the word "rain," on one part of the causal explanation of the bow. This profound causal connection to the rain is missing from the mathematical French term, which names only the arc and points out that it is an arc in the sky, *l'arc-en-ciel.* The differences between *"arc"* and "bow," "sky" *(ciel)* and "rain," and between either of these French or English terms and the earlier word "Iris," make clear the fact that naming always remembers only certain details about an object, thrusting them to the front whenever we want to think about it at all, with certain lines of thought already favored, the table tilted even before thought begins to roll. The presence of rain in the English word rainbow and in the German *Regenbogen* thrusts a key fact of the ultimate explanation into our field of vision whenever we think of the problem. The French language sets into prominence a different but equally important detail—the mathematical word for a part of a circle, an arc.

Why does the rainbow turn up in an aside within Socrates' remark at this moment of describing the relation of philosophy to wonder? Why does philosophy seem to remind Socrates of two things from which all modern descriptions of philosophy would forcibly separate it: on the one hand from empirical science, that is, from the geometry, optics, and color theory that make up the explanation of the rainbow, and, on the other hand, from mythology, from explanations that fall back on the gods? In the nineteenth century Comte proposed three stages of human progress. Mankind has passed, he claimed, from religion and mythology, through the middle stage of philosophy, and has finally arrived at genuine science. For Socrates the three stages are called up simultaneously within the strange afterthought which follows and completes, by a process of aside, the famous definition: philosophy begins in wonder.

Equally odd is the question of why Socrates distracts us from *arche* (origin) to *geneologein* (to the genealogy of a word, its etymology or source). Why does he do this in giving Theaetetus, who is confused in his attempt to understand a complex philosophical problem, an example of a small moment of explanation, a satisfactory moment of puzzle and solution, in giving him the genealogical explanation of the word Thaumas? Surely this type of explanation of things by means of the explanation of words is the worst possible model for intellectual or philosophical explanation. Only if Socrates believes that long ago, when the words were first chosen, the deep interconnections of things were seen clearly and built into language can his interest in the families of words make philosophical sense. If this were his belief, then we must assume that we have now forgotten these relations, but that careful work on the roots within words will bring the now buried relations back to light. How can Socrates turn our attention with his casual word "and" from Theaetetus' philosophical problems and confusion, which are the perfect instance for being "lost in wonder," to the gods, the rainbow, to explanation by family genealogy (daughter of) and by the genealogy, or as we would say, etymology, of words?

The remarkable cluster of submerged and tangential energies that surround, in Socrates' mind, the impulse that produced the always quoted fragment "Philosophy begins in wonder" are now clear. Philosophy, wonder, the father-daughter relation, the rainbow and the gods, the generational relations of both men and words, the *arche* or first stage of things: might these be no more than an accident of context or, even worse, a clear sign that at this moment there was an informal pause in the argument itself, a dramatic moment for the play of personality and intellectual relief while the concentrated powers needed to go on with the argument were rested for a moment? Do we have here the play of thought—Socrates relaxed—and not the work of thought?

The cluster of energies is at least not unique to this moment of Socratic argument. The analysis of Socrates' sentence could be taken as an outline of the philosophically profound account of wonder in Shakespeare's *Tempest,* his greatest play governed by and addressed to the passion of wonder. The play is named for and begins with a highly localized storm that sows confusion among a crew who will be lost and scattered until explanation binds them, at last, together. Just as every local storm makes possible a rainbow, *The Tempest* builds in a masque whose two main characters are Iris and Ceres, the rainbow and the generative goddess of wheat and harvest. At the play's core is a father, Prospero, who is a *Thaumaturge,* a producer of wonders, and his daughter Miranda, named for wonder *(Mira).* The daughter's name calls attention to the fact that it is in the ordinary act of sexual generation that a wonder (the child) is produced that is greater than any of the magician's tricks of storms and confusion. Miranda is both the play's object or goal (a young woman on the verge of marriage) and the incarnation of the state of wonder in the face of everything that occurs around her. She is to be wondered at (Mira-*nda*) and she is the passionate state itself.

The play leads towards sexual generation and marriage, but its subject, located in the transition from the father-daughter relation to the relation between man and wife, is the intergenerational replacement in which an erasure of anger and revenge first becomes possible without any act of forgiveness or vengeance. The erasure can be that of a child simply never knowing what has taken place—Miranda's condition before her father at last tells her his story—or it can equally be the ordinary, simple erasure that takes place in every act of forgetting. His story, once she knows it, does not govern all or even many of her subsequent acts or feelings. Either solution is a profound intergenerational fact tied to the fresh possibility, for the young, that the world is new, as yet unseen, unmarked by the experience of others. Ferdinand, who for her father is his enemy's son, is for Miranda the first and only man her own age that she has ever seen. Within this intergenerational forgetting the opportunity for wonder occurs.

The years in which Shakespeare wrote *The Tempest* (roughly 1610–11) are the years that, in science, are marked by the work of Kepler and by Galileo's invention of the telescope in 1609, which brought, as Galileo claimed, more new wonders into experience than any discovery in human history. The unknown silent majority of the stars could at last be seen. The moons of Jupiter were seen for the first time, letting the earth with its circling moon and its own motions of rotation and revolution around the sun be seen, by analogy, for the first time. *The Tempest* was written within a few years of Kepler's solution of the elliptical orbits of the planets around the sun—his laws of motion—and Galileo's key works.

After Kepler's, a much more modest watershed in science occurred with Descartes's work on the rainbow in 1637, the optical work of Huygens, and, finally, Newton's theory of color in the 1660s. In combination Descartes and Newton solved the fundamental questions of the rainbow. Newton considered his work on color, the proof that white is a blend of all colors and can be decomposed into a rainbow-like array of colors that can then be blended again to make white light, to be his greatest achievement.

At every stage of cosmology when the sun and stars, the planets and the earth were newly comprehended, but also newly experienced as remote and sublime objects, one sublunar, but still celestial object, the rainbow, translated down into an almost human scale the mystery and beauty, but also the search for exact mathematical explanation, which scored its more sublime, periodic successes up among the stars. The rainbow was always, whether in mythology or science, understood to be the one part of heaven that occurred here on earth, just over there, touching a neighbor's barn and that familiar tree, in front of the hill, closer than the nearest town. At each stage of almost ungraspable cosmic thought, that contemplation of infinite space that made Pascal dizzy with fear, the companionable earthly neighbor, the rainbow focused and domesticated, as it came to be re-wondered and investigated, the scientific delight that, in the inhuman realm of the sun and stars, always had an edge of fear.

The rainbow had been a central problem of science from the time of Aristotle's work on meteorology—his study of all things below the moon—through the work of Newton in 1669–1671, or to carry the story further, until the work of the happily named British scientist George Airy, who in the mid-nineteenth century made the last important synthesis within the theory of the rainbow. Again and again in the history of science a new method within science has been illustrated by a classic treatise on the rainbow. Aristotle begins this sequence, followed by Roger Bacon, Grosseteste, and finally Descartes, whose most important work, usually taken to inaugurate modern philosophy, the *Discourse on Method,* was originally the preface to three works illustrating his new method. The eighth section of the second of these works, *Meteors,* was his solution to the rainbow.

Descartes, who called his section on the rainbow the key demonstration of his new method, also wrote, a decade later in his final book, the most significant modern work on the passions. Descartes's book set the inner world free from its Aristotelian and scholastic terms, providing a new description of human nature, one that had as the first and central passion, the passion of wonder. The seventeenth century of Kepler, Galileo, Descartes, and Newton, this century of space and motion, was also the period of the most profound reflection on the passions since the writings of Plato, Aristotle, and the Stoics. Descartes and Spinoza refocused the theory of the passions in ways that made it a psychology for a civilization of science (Descartes) and for modern secular existence under conditions of power and violence (Spinoza and Hobbes). Descartes's new philosophy of the passions might be said to restate Socrates' "Philosophy begins in wonder" as "Human existence begins in wonder."

What I have introduced so far and will work out in detail in the pages that follow is the interplay between what we might call the psychology of scientific discovery as it was bound up with an exact description of the passion of wonder and, on the other hand, the poetics of thought, the participation of aesthetics, science, and philosophy in a common domain of the spirit, a domain that is firmly anchored to the exploitation of the epistemology of youth, or "newness" as it might better be called, and closely tied to a notion of rationality that includes the energy of the passions. What follows is a meditation on the phrase "All philosophy has its origin in wonder."

Visual Experience: Wonder and the Ordinary

When we think of the Seven Wonders of the World we realize at once that wonder is a relation to the visible world. Wonder is the outcome of the fact that we see the world. Only the visual is instantaneous, the entire object and all its details present at once. If we approach something with our eyes closed we make possible an instant of time in which the full effect of the object can, as we say, strike us. Yet even here we describe a situation in which we expected something to be wonderful and that is why we have been told to close our eyes. For the full experience of wonder there must be no description beforehand that will lead us to compare what we actually experience with what we were told, or even with the level of expectation raised by the one who told us to close our eyes. The object must be unexpectedly, instantaneously seen for the first time. In classical literature one of the most important tropes of wonder was the sudden appearance in a woods, just as one turns on the path, of a woman so beautiful that without reflection the exclamation "Dea certe!" (Certainly a goddess!) escapes from the mouth. The words seem unwilled; no reflection or pause takes place in which to compare the woman's beauty or grace to that of other women so as to quantify just how much more beautiful she must be to count not just as the most beautiful woman ever seen, but instead, surely, as a goddess.

The idea of a first-time experience is just as important as the first instant of sight to the experience of wonder. The second appearance of the woman or goddess on the same path, or anywhere else, would only lead to finding her as beautiful as before. She can only out-leap all of our categories of experience once. For wonder there must be no element of memory in the experience. That is part of the purity of this involuntary and, at least at first, purely aesthetic experience, an experience of the senses. Memory and, as a result of memory, expectation, presume the part of the will within experience, the search for and creation of experience. Wonder in its first moment stands outside the will. The devaluation of memory, or rather the closer connection of aesthetic, purely sensory experience, to wonder and, therefore, to intellectual life, is one of the most unexpected details of the experience.

The first sight of Frank Lloyd Wright's Fallingwater House in the woods of Pennsylvania, with the white geometry of the house set over a waterfall, is one of the best modern aesthetic experiences designed in advance to be an experience of wonder. For that reason it is not a house to be lived in, where daily return after work could only make banal its design, which is meant to strike the mind by its unexpectedness. Its real architectural effect is felt by the many visitors who come, for the first time, around the bend in the woods and have the house there in front of them for an instant of time.

The man who works near the pyramids and sees them every day finds them to be a mundane feature of his world. On the other hand, if we had never seen the sky, the sun, the night filled with stars, the earth covered with snow, these now commonplace things would stop us in our tracks with wonder and draw from us that modern equivalent of "Dea certe!" the simple exclamation of a prolonged "Ah!"

But, as it is, three things work against our ability to feel wonder in the face of just those primary facts that, when we are able to remind ourselves intellectually of their strangeness and beauty, dwarf at once the actual objects left over for wonder just because of their rarity and the accident of their being, for us, new experiences. These two conditions impose on us the relatively secondary experiences of the pyramids or Wright's Fallingwater house as our basic examples of the experience of wonder. First; the sun, the stars at night, snow, a blazing fire and all of the most visually striking experiences of our world are part of the common furniture of daily life. They are not rare experiences. Wonder is one category within the aesthetics of rare experiences.

The sun, fire, and snow are also part of the realm of expected, or regularly recurrent experiences, and wonder has its elemental existence in surprise. But these two features of rarity and unexpectedness are only part of the barrier. Even more important is the fact that our first experiences, our first sight of the sun, snow, fire, the stars at night took place in infancy or early childhood at a time when everything was unexpected because there was not yet in place that fundamental feature of mature experience, the idea of an ordinary world. Because we lacked the background of the normal, the banal, the always present, the regularly recurrent, the ordinary look of this or that—in short, the commonplace—at the moment of our first experiences of snow or fire these things were no more extraordinary than a new red mitten or someone who knew how to whistle.

This aesthetic paradox—that wonder depends on first sight and first experience and yet by the time that we are old enough to have the experience of wonder we may have already used up and dulled by repetition all of the most significant potential experiences of the truly wonderful—will play a fundamental part later in this argument. I only mention it here.

Since wonder declines with age, as Descartes pointed out, it is a basic experience of youth, but only of youth far enough along into the familiarity of the ordinary world to be able to see against this background the truly unexpected, the truly beautiful. Are we left, once we are ready for wonder, with only the poor cousins of just those experiences that happened to us long before the structure of "having an experience" existed at all?

Wittgenstein in the *Brown Notebook* discusses a question that makes this relation of wonder to the ordinary clear.[4] He asks what the ordinary feels like. Is there really a feeling at all? What he means is this. Can we recognize or notice that, for example, this is my ordinary shoe? Is it only if something is wrong with it, let us say that it has been stolen or replaced with a different shoe or had paint spilled onto it or lost its heel, that I can "notice" it? Can I notice just the simple fact that it is my ordinary shoe? Is it only defect or change within the ordinary that lets consciousness enter at all? Heidegger in his well-known analysis of the world of tools claims that it is only if the hammer is missing or broken or no longer seems aligned when we strike a nail that we become conscious of it or even look at it, as opposed to using it without the act of attending to it.

Wittgenstein's point is that there can be no "feeling of the ordinary." The shoe is just there where it ought to be or functioning without my attention until or unless something takes it out of the ordinary. What Wittgenstein contrasts to the ordinary is the feeling of surprise. Clearly this is a feeling. We notice something in so far as it is unexpected. Wittgenstein is producing a variant of the classical analysis of wonder as we find it, for example, in Descartes. What Descartes means by wonder *(l'admiration)* is the act of noticing with pleasure something new and unprecedented. The act of noticing in and of itself gives pleasure. But for Descartes the act of being able to notice something requires that it be unexpected, not part of the ordinary. The two words taken together cover the temporal and the spatial details of the experience. In time what happens was not expected; in space it was not ordinary. It was not always already there.

Descartes, too, would say that we cannot have a feeling of the ordinary; or what is slightly different, we cannot have an experience of the ordinary. By feeling or experience here we mean that we have a definable moment of a special kind that might be noticed, remembered, formulated in description, something discrete within the flow of time, something clear, self-contained, separable from what came before and after. This would be a patch of experience, a *this* with its own duration and quality.

To characterize wonder we are forced to look at its alternative, the qualities of the ordinary, and paradoxically what we end up saying is that there cannot be any experience of the ordinary. As a result, surprise, the eliciting of notice, become the very heart of what it means to "have an experience" at all. There does not necessarily exist an experience of both alternatives: an experience of surprise and an experience of the ordinary. This is important for the idea of wonder. The ordinary can not or does not turn itself into experiences. The ordinary is what is there when there are no experiences going on. It is the necessary optics within which there can be such a thing as an experience, but which cannot itself be seen. We can see a cell within a microscope, but never a microscope.

One definition of the ordinary would be that which is not being seen for the first time. The importance of first sight within the experience of wonder opens up the connection between aesthetics and thought, particularly in the problem of discovery. This too will be spelled out in detail later in this argument, but for now it is enough to say that from the start wonder was recognized as a philosophical experience. Being struck by something is exactly opposite to being struck dumb. The tie between wonder and learning is clear in the moment when after long confusion and study you suddenly say, "Now I get it!" Plato, in an example that I will look at in detail later, uses mathematics for this because the moment of "getting it" is extremely clear in mathematics. In an instant, unexpectedly, the answer is seen for the first time, and all that was a puzzle of unrelated facts up to that instant turns into clarity and order. The experience of discovery cannot be repeated. When we go back over the steps of the problem, the solution that surprised us when we first saw it is now just one more obvious step.

Wonder and learning are tied by three things: by suddenness, by the moment of first seeing, and by the visual presence of the whole state or object. So important is the visual, the sudden, and the unexpected within the experience of wonder that within the arts wonder is almost uniquely possible within architecture, sculpture, painting, and within grand projects of engineering like the George Washington Bridge where, in every case, a sudden experience of the whole is possible. The arts of time—narration, dance, and music—are never present as a whole in an instant of time. They also depend on controlled expectation followed by surprise against the background of what we have been led to think will happen next. Wonder does not depend on awakening and then surprising expectation, but on the complete absence of expectation. Memory and expectation are so fundamental to the narrative arts and, usually, to music that wonder is ruled out, or is replaced, we might say, by mere surprise, as in a twist of plot. Only in occasional cases does a temporal art even court the possibilities of the unexpected and the sudden that open up the aesthetics of wonder.

The music of Stravinsky might be the best example, because in Stravinsky the instantaneous effects, the strangeness of the combination of instruments and sounds, the sudden introduction of elements without preparation, the rapid changes of tempo and rhythm work in the end to create pure moments of beauty and surprise that seek the response "Ah!" Bach, Mozart, or Jane Austen are more normative for the part played by repetition, variation, expectation, and the play of promise and satisfaction within the arts of time. For someone who has never seen one before, the first experience of a painting by Jackson Pollock or of a sculpture by Giacometti, for which even the widest knowledge of earlier painting or sculpture is no preparation, is in its essence an experience of wonder.

Lyric poetry has always, among the arts of time, had uniquely potent means to reach out for the effects of wonder that are more at home in the visual. In language it is the work of familiar syntactic structures and the work of grammar that builds in a strong component of expectation at every moment. When we hear "I saw the . . ." we know before the next word appears that it will almost certainly be a noun because "saw" needs a direct object and the word "the" tells us that a noun will soon appear. These small scale syntactic and grammatical expectations are nested within other structures of ever larger scale which are fundamental to narrative itself, with expectation controlled and played with at every stage. "When I saw the fallen tree, I quickly steered the car into the other lane while watching to avoid the oncoming traffic." Syntax and grammar are the enemies of wonder, no less than the large number of typical, everyday narrative story types that we always know that we are about to hear one new variation within, as the sentence above illustrates.

In the arts of time what we call the narrative aspect is just the sequence of details, drawn together by syntax into a set of stressed relations. One after another the details are presented for attention in a sequence determined by the author or by the director in a film. By contrast, in all-at-once visual experiences like wonder, all details are present at once. We first take in the whole. The next step of the experience, for any viewer, is to create her own narrative, by looking now at this detail, then at that, changing scale to larger or smaller details, inventing in each experience a self-determined history of attention.

The exploratory freedom of this attention as it plays over the details, instead of receiving them one after another as the sentences of the novel or the shots of the film determine, makes up a self-determined narration of the wealth of details in the aftermath of the first instant of wonder. Narrative is not absent in the visual. Instead, control over it has passed from the artist to the viewer. The tyranny of narrative attention is one of the most ethically complex issues in literature. The encouraged freedom of the visual arts, the need to begin to attend now to this, now to that, opens up a channel of affiliation between visual wonder and thought and closes down that same channel between thought and narration in the arts of time.

The clear authority of the visual and only the visual is one of the great themes of Cartesian method. The aesthetics of the visual, no less than the science of visual—algebraic representations, diagrams, and geometry—has anchored all thinking about aesthetics to the extent that it is something of a tautology to speak about the aesthetics of the visible.

Modern poetry since Mallarmé has weakened the part played by grammar and syntax and crossed a critical threshold in the use—one after another—of unexpected words and references until expectation itself ceases to work and the experience of wonder can take over. However, within language, because we expect grammar and syntax, any such experience of wonder can feel to most people like an annoying obscurity rather than a pleasure. Mallarmé's "Le Tombeau de Baudelaire" could be called a test case for the possibility of wonder within the arts of time. Since an example in English is easier to consider, the following lines of T. S. Eliot show how this weakening of syntax and the use of the surprising word anesthetizes the part played by expectation in temporal art.

> Garlic and sapphires in the mud
> Clot the bedded axle-tree.
> The trilling wire in the blood
> Sings below inveterate scars . . .[5]

One detail of these lines is the crowding of nouns, of thing words, so that a whirl occurs in the mind because we have too many balls in the air, too many things, too few relations among them. Even the words that should relate the nouns turn out also to bring up new nouns and things, like the verb "clot" which is also a noun, or the modifier "bedded" which brings in the noun "bed." The fused word "axle-tree" in which two diverse nouns are soldered together gives us a model for the poem as a whole: many nouns held together by a set of invisible hyphens.

After a certain number of things in unclear relation or weak relation, the temporal becomes the visual and the whole set of objects hangs in space before the mind, like a visual diagram. Connectives that should link similar things—boys *and* girls, salt *and* pepper—are used for radically different things—garlic *and* sapphires. No relation is proposed except to juxtapose them to a third thing by saying that they are *in* the mud. The weak or unexpected uses of *and* and *in* here show the style of reaching the visual by suspending the machinery that narrativizes the objects. By the third line we have garlic, sapphires, mud, clot, bed, axle, tree, wire, and blood. Syntax has vanished and along with syntax, narrative. Wonder is now possible.

It is not only the obscurity of modern poetry that demonstrates how the lyric can produce the spatial crowding that is a condition for wonder; the simple lines of a song of Shakespeare's can show how poetry brings together the effects of surprise, suddenness, and the moment of wonder.

> Golden lads and girls all must,
> As chimney-sweepers, come to dust.[6]

The Instant of Wonder and the Instant of Thought

Vladimir Nabokov in his early novel *The Gift* describes and mimetically isolates the stages of an experience of wonder. He describes his hero in the street.

> As he crossed toward the pharmacy at the corner he involuntarily turned his head because of a burst of light that had ricocheted from his temple, and saw, with that quick smile with which we greet a rainbow

or a rose, a blindingly white parallelogram of sky being unloaded from the van—a dresser with mirror across which, as across a cinema screen, passed a flawlessly clear reflection of boughs sliding and swaying not arboreally, but with a human vacillation, produced by the nature of those who were carrying this sky, these boughs, this gliding façade.[7]

In this remarkable, single long sentence Nabokov recreates for the reader the narrative surprise along with its momentarily delayed explanation. Within that modern essence of the ordinary and the everyday—crossing a street, out on a chore—attention is summoned suddenly and unexpectedly—the hero involuntarily turned his head because of a burst of light that had ricocheted off his temple. The ballistic word "ricocheted" suggests being shot by the burst of light. He is called out to by the light as he might have been by a shout—"Watch out!" His life interrupted, his head turned involuntarily, wonder begins—the "quick smile" that sees the "white parallelogram of sky" being unloaded from the dark inside of a moving van. Then inside the syntax of an explanatory dash, in effect an aside, we recognize (as he does) a dresser with a mirror being carried by movers out of the van. Immediately the mind jumps to an analog—a movie screen—then returns to pleasure—this sky, these boughs, this glittering façade.

Each mentioned instance of wonder—rainbow, rose, parallelogram of sky emerging from a van, cinema screen—occurs within the ordinary and the everyday, and once explained it is itself part of that everyday. Unlike the "Dea certe!" experience, this modern instance assumes the domestication of aesthetic categories like wonder and the part played by the accidental and extremely short-lived unique moment of beauty: just now and never again will the world give me this to look at, a quirky moment, mine alone. Nabokov's two analogs, rainbow and rose, are classes of events, brief, experienced by many, rare but not singular, as true anywhere in the world, thousands of years ago, thousands of years hence, while dressers with mirrors, moving vans, and so on are part of the furniture of a few cultural places, and never existed at all before modern times. The experience itself is just for a time—like piano rolls, or indoor electrical lamps.

At first the experience may even seem to depend on that most depressing cycle of enchantment/disenchantment. "It's *only* a dresser," we might say. Stendhal made famous the aesthetics of "N'est-ce que ça?"—Is that all it is? These are nothing but banal household furnishings, a dresser with a mirror. Yet the everyday has been shuffled and displaced. The sky is down here, coming out of a van. For Nabokov the explanation does not deflate the wondrous. It might only seem to do so for a brief second part way through the experience. Surprise and the unexpected do play a key role in the experience initially, but a second kind of delight, a wonder not predicated on surprise, ends the sentence, which has three phases and not the simple pair of enchantment and disenchantment, pleasure and its collapse into recognition.

It is essential that the event described is a visual all-at-once experience. What narrative adds to that experience is the sequence of recognitions that took place in fractions of a second of time. The first of these—that quick smile with which we greet a rainbow or a rose—instructs us, by setting rainbow and rose in front of us before we even know what the experience is, to respond in a certain way. We ask inwardly, because the structure postpones its object for a micro-second, just what could bring the same pleasure as an unexpected rainbow or rose? Nabokov's syntax unfolds these stages from partial knowledge (a white rectangle of sky), to recognition (a dresser with a mirror), to association (a movie screen), and finally to a state of prolonged pleasure as we enjoy and prolong the sight of the swaying boughs (a metonymy of excitement and pleasure) and the final image of men carrying and with their motion animating and exciting the sky, boughs, and façade.

In the end we replace the first delighted smile by a return to mysterious pleasure dependent on leaving out, in the final phrase, the word reflection. The hero forgets, or rather is so taken by the literal event in front of him that he reports only what he sees—men carrying "this sky, these boughs, this glittering façade," not men carrying a mirror that reflected "this sky, these boughs, this glittering façade."

Many elements of wonder are here: the sudden, the unexpected, the all-at-once of the visual, a first-time experience, a rare or even singular event, a progression from mystification to explanation, a feeling of the freshness of the world, the bodily states of the smile and the swaying—a somatic pleasure much like the state that Wordsworth experienced in the field of dancing daffodils.

Nabokov's urban moment should not be confused with the type of case that underlies our theory of metaphor—that we make things strange by means of language, that we renew (re-new) what is not in fact new by figuration or by that stronger modern rhetorical device, configuration. The sky that comes out of the moving van is a fragile but literal experience.

Even within ordinary visual experiences we can bring about, by means of willful thought, the production of at least a simulation of wonder. Nabokov, a few pages later in *The Gift*, describes the moving van's disappearance. "The van had gone and in the spot where its tractor had recently stood, there remained next to the sidewalk a rainbow of oil, with the purple predominant and a plumelike twist. Asphalt's parakeet."[8] The iridescent oil itself is not the marvel here; rather, it is the use of metaphor—a "rainbow" of oil and then, even more fancifully, "asphalt's parakeet." The parakeet is not seen but imagined, associated, cleverly joined, oil and bird, gutter and sky, a fancy and I would say "forced" or "constructed" marvel. The words call attention not to the scene itself but to the cleverness of the mind that associated it with a parakeet. We feel about Nabokov here what we feel when we see that Picasso could see the seat and handlebars of a bicycle as the head of a bull. What is striking in both cases is the wit of the artist, not the essence of the event. In the phrase "asphalt's parakeet" we can factor out the modern distinction between seeing and seeing as: seeing as a rainbow, seeing as a parakeet. With the dresser and mirror we are speaking only of seeing. Of the visual, not the gaudy metaphoric.

The intellectual mechanism of wonder stands apart from the aesthetic idea of estrangement or defamiliarization, the romantic notion first proposed by Novalis as the key to Romantic poetics, that art is a way of making an object strange or alien. Coleridge took over the idea when he spoke of making the familiar strange, one half of his and Wordsworth's project in the *Lyrical Ballads*. The aesthetics of modern culture, including Brecht and Surrealism, has depended on this key idea, repeated in the modern period by the Russian Formalist Sklovski as *Ostranyi.*

Wonder has only superficial similarities to estrangement. The central example of the rainbow should make this clear: it is the rare and compelling object itself, not some jaded renewal of it by estrangement, that is productive of attention. Estrangement has everything to do with the problem of boredom, with overfamiliarity, with the dull effects of habit. These are key nineteenth-century aesthetic problems to which the invention of willed estrangement was proposed as an answer. Wonder is not one more episode in the aesthetic history of boredom.

Nor is wonder connected to shock. Surprise is, in its quiet, thoughtful way, less melodramatic than shock, less radical. Nabokov's mirror unloaded from a van is an instance of the effect of surprise from things being "out of place"—one of the classic effects within modernism. But in Nabokov's example we are taken back to the essence of mirrors: something over there appears over here. Ordinarily, the dresser stands all day in the same place in the bedroom. We see it each day with the very same rectangle from across the room reflected in its surface. The dresser in the street on moving day, jiggling as it is carried, not in its ordinary place and moving rather than at rest, capturing an ever-changing image like a cinema screen but now inverting the situation because it is the screen that is moving and not the film—this combination makes available for thought the fact of reflection and its conditions in a remarkable way.

Yet even here we cannot say that we discover anything new about these relationships. We remember them, we have them back in consciousness, rather than in the background. The unloaded mirror shares with Novalis's romantic aesthetic the central goal of recovering what we already know, rather than discovering, the goal of bringing into consciousness the conditions of daily life, the repressed, the habitual, or the forgotten script in which events take place.

None of these cases leads to learning, and they are not, in Descartes's sense, an attention to something new. For this reason Nabokov's moving dresser and mirror, while pleasurable, are not a full instance of philosophical wonder.

If we consider briefly another literary description of a visual experience, the missing center of Nabokov's urban moment will be clear.

Dante's *Paradiso* is the longest sustained poem of wonder in literature. As the first writer to "see" and describe the universe from outside the limits of the earth, to give as a traveler or visitor the first and only human account of paradise, Dante imbues his poem with one long succession of *ammerazione*—wonders. But among these many, almost incommunicable visual wonders, the second canto sets out a modest, very human scientific moment that could stand for the essence of the idea of wonder that will be at stake in this book.

Beatrice, in trying to answer Dante's questions about the disk of the moon, tells him to try an experiment. He is to see for himself.

> Taking three mirrors, place a pair of them
> at equal distance from you; set the third
> midway between those two, but farther back.
>   Then, turning toward them, at your back have placed
> a light that kindles those three mirrors and
> returns to you, reflected by them all.
>   Although the image in the farthest glass
> will be of lesser size, there you will see
> that it must match the brightness of the rest.[9]

In this truly remarkable moment we have an extremely complicated physical array whose only purpose is to make a moment of visual simultaneity possible. The poet is to sit facing three mirrors, with the middle one much farther away than those on either side of it. Behind him, and therefore invisible to him, is a candle. In the three mirrors, his glance can see two things, both of which depend on the idea of equality. First, the size of the reflection of the candle in the mirror farther away is smaller, or not equal to the other two. Second, the brightness, the quantity of light from the middle image, is equal to the other two.

In this modest moment Beatrice has arranged an "all-at-once" visual moment of surprise, certainty, and learning. Every detail has been made, through the artifice of the experiment, locally simultaneous and visible.

The simple fact of discovery *is* present when Beatrice describes the three mirrors that Dante is asked to face with the middle one twice as far away from him as the two that flank it right and left. In the instant when he sees that the size of the candle flame in the two nearer mirrors is twice that of the flame in the more distant mirror, but that the brightness is the same, he will have factored or separated out two aspects of the light—size and intensity—so that in a glance he learns the separability of the two—the constancy of brightness in spite of the change of size with distance. Dante will in this moment have faced a surprising, exact visual event, and as a result of surprise, he will have learned. The learning will be remembered just because of the memorable physical event with its attendant pleasure and surprise.

To add one key layer to this analysis I want to consider a third instance, the Hellenistic example of the refraction of light, a small experiment that also uses the deep surprise of the visual, a simple experiment that, correctly understood, explains many of the deepest problems of vision. The experiment, in Michel Authier's description, is this: "Take a vase and place a coin at the bottom so that when the vase rests on a table you can still see the coin at the bottom. Now slide the vase away from you until the coin just disappears as your line of sight is blocked by the side of the vase. Now fill the vase with water. You will see the coin once again, because of the bending of rays of light, their refraction in the medium of water."[10]

This small surprise, a visible proof of refraction, was fundamental not because of the everyday domestic facts of table, vase, coin, and water but because, as Authier describes it: "If you substitute for the water, the atmosphere above us; for the vase the sky; and for the small object the sun or any one of the stars, you will have a model for the basic phenomenon of all astronomy: the refraction of light, the difference between apparent location and true location."

In this tiny experiment the first surprise—seeing the object once the water has been poured into the vase—is a moment of pleasure and wonder, but the second surprise—that this table-top experiment replicates and helps us understand the sky, the stars, light moving through our atmosphere, which we are asked to recognize as a medium like the water in the vase—this second surprise of analogy—is an intellectual one.

Why do we use this type of demonstration for the idea of refraction rather than referring to an everyday event—a stick that appears bent when we see it half in, half out of a pond? The vase creates an experience (an event-moment) of visual surprise, a moment of the unexpected, that clearly produces in the aftermath of pleasure a curiosity that asks: how did that happen? It is a repeatable experience—we can use another vessel, another object, repeat it tomorrow, use the floor rather than the table. As we do these things the link between pleasure and investigation, or rather the process by which pleasure induces, converts into, and then sustains investigation, is clear. An aesthetic component appears in the moments of surprise and delight, and in the instantaneous, visual moment within understanding. The mind says "Aha!" in the aesthetic moment when the spirit says "Ah!"

Yet in this case, as in the experiment of the three mirrors in Dante, the event has been staged. We know that the discoveries themselves were *not* made by someone who just happened to be contemplating a coin in a jug or a room with a chair, a candle, and three mirrors. The artificiality of the circumstances tips us off. These are demonstrations, or more precisely, *stagings,* by someone who knows and earlier learned the idea in some other way, for learners who are to be shown the effect in this dramatic way. These are melodramas of instruction and not acts of discovery. They involve the ironic structure of wonder in a profound way—the dramatic irony that is produced by the differing frames of knowledge of the one who tells us to look (Beatrice) and the one who, without knowing the reason for this artificial structure, undergoes the experiment (Dante).

What I am calling subjectivity here is the horizon of what is, *for me,* at this point of my life, the ordinary, the everyday, and the common. "O, wonder! / How many goodly creatures are there here! / How beauteous mankind is! O brave new world / That has such people in't!" (5.1. 182–184) exclaims Miranda in *The Tempest,* in one of the classical passages of wonder. "'Tis new to thee" retorts her father, Prospero, who sees nothing new or wondrous in the pack of human scoundrels in front of his eyes. Miranda, however, has known only her father and Caliban, the superhuman and the subhuman, and she has, as a result of the shipwreck, now seen humanity, young and old, multiple and in some variety, for the first time.

𝒯he Rainbow and Cartesian Wonder

The Aesthetics of the Rainbow

This first sketch of the experience of wonder now makes it possible to show in detail why the rainbow is a central instance of the aesthetics of wonder. Why it is also central in that zone where science touches or overlaps with aesthetics is a question that still has to be postponed. As I will attempt to show later, wonder does not enter within science only in the elegance or beauty of results, but far more essentially in the detailed psychology of how discovery happens, the step-by-step practice of thought. Before reaching this poetics of thought, for which the rainbow will also provide a central instance, I want to work out the plausibility of the rainbow as an equally central instance within the aesthetics of wonder.

In the aesthetics of experience the rainbow stands alongside many other candidates for wonder, for example, the night sky filled with stars. The stars, like Wordsworth's description of what he called "the world," are "too much with us." They return night after night, the same in their slow dance of variation, returning seasonally and in larger cycles to the same configurations. Emerson pointed out, "If the stars should appear one night in a thousand years, how would men believe and adore; and preserve for many generations the remembrance of the city of God which had been shown."[1] We have or can have too much experience of the stars. Scientifically, the stars led at once to the study of repetition, not uniqueness. We could say that the patterns of the stars led to the very idea of scientific lawfulness: regularity and, therefore, the predictability of future states.

By contrast, the rainbow is, in every individual life, a rare experience, and it is always a sudden and an unexpected one. Most people know that a rainbow has to do with rain, with the sun, and with a sky partially darkened by clouds against which the rainbow appears. The rain showers must be local. If the sky were completely cloudy the sun could not be out, providing the light source. Some know that no rainbow can occur when the sun is above a certain height in the sky, or that rainbows are most likely in late afternoon or in the morning when the sun is relatively low. Most realize that the rainbow is opposite the sun and that to see it we stand with our backs to the sun facing the semicircle of bands of color, always red in the outer band, green in the middle, blue in the inner band.

This knowledge seldom lets us anticipate the experience. As a result, each experience of the rainbow is sudden, unexpected and widely separated in time from our last most recent instance. While the rainbow is rare, it is still common enough to have been named, thought about, and to have entered most people's individual experience as an experience. Objects that are too rarely seen never stabilize themselves in human language at all with the privilege of a name, or, worse, their very reality is disputed since most people have never seen them even once. Aristotle, for example, points out that there are very rare instances of moon rainbows, too rare for us to have an exact term or name for these white, ghostlike objects. Aristotle claimed that there could not be more than two occurrences of moon rainbows in fifty years. In his classic history of the scientific explanation of the rainbow, Carl Boyer points out why these are so rare.

> For one thing, the large majority of local showers, over land areas where most people live, occur in the summer afternoon when the moon has no chance to produce a bow. Then, too, the full moon would appear to the east of the observer during the early hours of the evening, whereas the prevailing winds in many regions are from the west and

hence make the eastern sky too cloudy for a bow. When one realizes that lunar rainbows occur about a hundredth as frequently as solar rainbows, and if one recollects that fully three-fourths of these will be missed through sleep, he will better appreciate the rarity of observations of lunar bows.[2]

The lunar bow is at the other extreme from the too often seen, too predictable night sky with stars. It is too rarely seen to have ever entered most people's experience even in an eighty-year lifetime. Experiences at this extreme are also ruled out for the aesthetics of wonder. The white lunar bow also falls short in lacking the striking beauty and differentiation of the red-green-blue bands of the rainbow. More a white smear across a sky, which in any case has the constant appearance of white in its clouds, the lunar rainbow cannot strike the eye and mind. The display of color in nature, as with brightly colored birds and flowers, has to do with attraction, most often with the sexual process itself. Color makes a claim for attention, a claim for love in its most elementary form as a combination of attraction and excitement. The rainbow strikes us, in a way that moon rainbows never could, even if they were common enough to be rare, just because it shares in the erotics of color, with color's reproductive force within nature.

The solar rainbow, in addition to the pleasures of color, of regularity, and of geometric form (the semicircle), has the great advantage of lasting only for a brief time. The precious transience that is one decisive part of most ideas of the experience of beauty, whether in Japan or in the Occident from the Greeks through the Renaissance to Romanticism, has its perfect instance in the rainbow, which lasts a few minutes only, long enough to be noticed and enjoyed, never so long as to outstay its welcome, so that, bored, we move on to look at something else. The sun, which hurts our eyes when we look directly at it, makes clear just how comfortable the rainbow's amount of light is for the capacities of human sight. The sun, unlike the rainbow, often hangs around the sky for twelve or fourteen hours at a time, too long to invite, reward, and then conclude the temporal side of what we call "having an experience."

Shorter-lived than flowers or the beauty of youth, those two primary examples of the relation of beauty to time, the rainbow localizes in its sudden disappearance, just as in its rare and unexpected arrival, the basic fact that beauty visits, never stays. Iris is the messenger of the gods. Insofar as wonder maps out the nature of experience itself, the vanishing no less than the unanticipated and sudden arrival of the rainbow mark out the just-long-enough of a time for one and only one experience.

Since beauty for the Greeks was mathematical, or to put it more strongly, since the geometrical and the proportional were the meeting point of aesthetics and science, as Pythagoras' work on harmony and proportion in music shows, the mystery of the arc of the rainbow, its half circle in a sky where clouds often appear in tatters, in all shapes and outlines, was, intellectually, the first of its qualities. The arc made the rainbow susceptible to geometry, and it was by means of geometrical reasoning that from Aristotle to Descartes and Newton, the rainbow was explained. Just as the rainbow drew and held attention, it seemed, in the geometrical regularity of its shape, to point out the path by which it could be understood. It solicited not only attention and interest, but the particular interest of those skilled in geometry.

Just as important an appeal to philosophy and thought as its semicircular shape was the fact that the rainbow was a phenomenon of light rather than of matter. This made it unique among the objects of beauty, noble in a way that the material beauty of flowers or of human faces could never be.

Finally, and most remarkably of all, from Aristotle on it was known that the rainbow involved subjectivity in a unique way. We each see the same sun, even if we stand on different hilltops. At night an observer in Boston and one in Havana who look into the sky each see the same stars in Orion's belt. But because the appearance of the rainbow is only possible by means of reflection, the angle between the observer, the sun, and the water droplets that reflect (and refract) the rays of light coming from the sun must be fixed for each observer. Two viewers see two different rainbows. A certain spot of red, for each of them, must come from a different drop of water, just that drop that stands in the right angular position between the observer and the sun. Each person's rainbow, like his or her reflection in a pool of water, is uniquely determined by the point where he or she stands, by the angle between eye, raindrop, and sun. If I try to approach the rainbow it moves further on.

Roger Bacon distinguished the real colors produced by light passing through a crystal and the rainbow: "The observer alone produces the bow, nor is there anything present except reflection. In the case of the crystal, however, there is a natural cause, namely, the ray and the corrugated stone, which has great diversity of surface, so that according to the angle at which the light falls a diversity of colors result. And viewing them does [not] cause the colours to be present here, for there is colour before it is seen here, and it is seen by different people in the same place. But in the case of the bow the phenomenon is the result of vision, and therefore can have no reality but mere appearance." [3] The great writer on optics Vitello pointed out the simple experiment of closing one eye and then the other while watching a small rainbow nearby in a spray of water. The rainbow changes its position depending on which eye is open. With this ingenious experiment we are able to simulate the experience of two different observers of the larger rainbow in the sky.

The rainbow that I see is like the horizon line, a mathematical artifact within experience. One consequence of this is that without human observers (or animal observers whose eyes work roughly similar to human eyes), there are no rainbows. They are part of the human world. On an uninhabited planet there would continue to be sun and rain, stars, and snow, but there would be no rainbow and no horizon. The horizon, a feature of experience which is always there, reminds us that the fate of the ordinary, no matter how striking once we are able to reflect on it, is to remain in the shadow of whatever is rare and sudden in experience, for example, the rainbow. In its requirement of a human observer to exist at all, rainbows and horizon lines are closer to music or geometry: had there been no human world there never would have been any such thing.

Noah's Rainbow and Religious Intelligibility

Taken together, the many characteristics of the rainbow described to this point make it clear why the rainbow could be taken as an epitome of an aesthetic experience, and more generally, as one unusually clear example of what we mean by "having an experience" at all. It is not clear why such an experience would elicit thought, a search for explanations and causes; that is, why it would elicit science rather than a stable self-contained delight.

Before I reach the poetics of thought, one alternative has to be mentioned that has in common with science a way of passing beyond the sensory or aesthetic experience, beyond the pleasure in the presence of the object of wonder. In the Bible, the rainbow is explained in the style of classic mythology by its origin, why it came to be there, after, presumably, a long period (antediluvian) when it did not exist. In the Bible the rainbow is placed in the sky by God, after the flood, as a sign—that is, as a token or reminder—of his promise never again to destroy the earth with water. "God gave Noah the rainbow sign. No more water, the fire next time," as the hymn puts it.

Mythological explanation narrativizes, or historicizes, the object to tell us three things about it: when it first came to exist (its genesis), who put it there, and why. This explanation turns it into a sign. It has passed from being an aesthetic object to being a meaningful object, a reminder. In looking at it at every later moment we are meant to think of something else (God's promise and God's wrath, man's sins, the one catastrophe that has been excluded). It is important to notice that this sign explanation tells us nothing about the sensory details of the rainbow, its colors, size, location in the sky, why double rainbows sometimes appear, what rainbows have to do with the height of the sun. The simple fact addressed is the connection of the rainbow to rain, to the end of a local shower. Implicitly, this explanation shows that what is being satisfied in this explanation is our fear, whenever rain starts, that it will never stop. The rainbow is met with relief in the collapse of a fear, which the story of God's promise fixes permanently into perception itself. Every rain as it starts brings on the imagination that it will go on and on, fill the rivers, cover the land, destroy everything.

Only one detail, the fact of rain, seen from the relief that the rain is a "local shower," which it must be for the sun to be out at the same time, has been brought to our attention to the exclusion of all other facts. This is the intellectual style of a world of fear, with its epistemological companion, fixed attention or obsession. The goal of the story (God–Noah–the flood–the rainbow–the promise) is to force the mind to pass as rapidly as possible from the aesthetic state to the state of memory (of this story, of human sinfulness). The essence of the aesthetic state of wonder is the play of the mind over the details of the object itself. Aesthetics is part of the mobility of attention, interest, and delight. Its lingering over the widest range of details so as to prolong its pleasurable contact with the object is one clue to the connection of wonder to science. In the attention brought about by wonder, the capacity to notice the actual details of the object is a strategy on the part of pleasure that seeks to last as long as possible. The substitution of fear and relief, the world of signs and meanings, just where aesthetic delight seems most spontaneously elicited, makes clear the connection of fear to memory and to a kind of obsessive, fixed focus of attention.

The religious meaning connected to the story of Noah, the flood, and God that leaps into the well-trained mind, distracts wonder, or to say it more strongly, preempts the possibility of wonder. The fear concealed within this story is not the fear of another flood, but the fear of wonder. The story is not accidentally attached to just this or that, it is positioned like a filter across just that experience that would elicit a lingering and free play of the mind, a delight and interest, a curiosity—in short, a combination of passion and energy, intellectual alertness and pleasure in the unknown that would itself lead on to science. The religious system of explanation is a technique in which beauty is wounded by meaning so that the work of wonder can never begin. To speak this way implies a deep hostility between narrative and aesthetic mobility and between meaning, in so far as meaning immobilizes attention, and aesthetic wonder and the exploratory curiosity that it sponsors.

From Wonder to Thought

What is made clear in the religious need to put this barrier across the path of wonder is the clear recognition, even within the religious system at war with this process, that rare objects of this kind, that lie at the heart of having an experience, elicit from us an activity. The aesthetic state is, only by a modern error, taken to be a passive one, a state of spectatorship rather than action. The activity is, of course, intellectual. More precisely, the aesthetic state as seen in the experience of wonder is the clearest miniature example of the details of thought itself, and this fact was recognized, as I will show in a number of examples, from the time of Plato to that of Descartes.

One important feature that follows from the aesthetic is that we do not have to seek out the things that we ought to think about scientifically. They strike us, as the stars do. They call attention to themselves against a background of things that do not spontaneously, on their own, call attention to themselves. This act of striking us makes up the figure-ground relation itself, as an active fact. The sudden appearance of the rainbow, its rareness, its beauty are all part of this initial act of striking us, trapping and holding our attention by means of beauty and the unwilled response of wonder. The "Ah!" of wonder is unreflective and immediate. It comes from us almost fast enough to say that it, too, surprises us. We learn a second later that we are already in the state of wonder. In this, wonder is like the other central passions—anger, fear, and grief—in that it involves a discovery about the limits of the will within experience, a location where we can no longer identify ourselves completely with our powers of choice, action, self-direction, and yet these territories of experience outside the will are intimately ourselves, uniquely determined, personal. Wonder begins with something imposed on us for thought.

The drive within wonder toward curiosity, questioning, and the search for explanation seems to involve no less than the religious move toward sign, history, memory, and meaning, a move away from the aesthetic experience itself, a passage from wonder to thinking. We know that thinking involves hard work, frustration, trial and error. It takes us through many moods of hope and impatience, disappointment, and even anger at the weakness of our powers of thought. Such feelings are not at all the simple continuation of the feeling of wonder. If wonder gives way to thought, does it stimulate in its delight in something only an aftermath of melancholy and hard work that are the more normal moods of thought? Does wonder inaugurate thought only to find itself displaced by radically different, nonaesthetic, dispassionate forms of activity? In other words, is science no different from religion in kidnapping the energy of wonder for an alien use and, in the end, even a use hostile to the energies of wonder itself?

What I will try to show in the next sections is that the passage from wonder to thought sets off a chain of experience built on ever repeated, small-scale repetitions of the experience of wonder. The first global moment of wonder is relocated, or better yet, reactivated, kept alive at every step within the process of thought itself. It is not the stimulus to thought, but the very core of energy that makes up each moment of thought. It is here, by means of Descartes and Plato, that we can see what is meant by the phrase "Philosophy begins in wonder." I will try to expand the saying to read: "Philosophy begins in wonder, continues on at every moment by means of wonder, and ends with explanation that produces, when first heard, a new and equally powerful experience of wonder to that with which it began." Wonder, in this sense, we can call the poetics of thought.

Descartes and the Scientific Passion of Wonder

The work of Descartes between 1630 and 1645 could stand as the unfolding of the remark of Socrates to Theaetetus: "This feeling of wonder shows that you are a philosopher, since wonder is the only beginning of philosophy, and he who said that Iris was the child of Thaumas made a good genealogy."[4] In these fifteen years that coincide with the condemnation of Galileo by the Inquisition and the attack on the Copernican system, Descartes made three Copernican revolutions of his own, overthrowing, as he claimed, all that had been done before. First, in his *Discourse on Method,* he wrote the key work that put an end to scholastic discussion and to the use of authorities like Aristotle or Aquinas within argument. Descartes begins modern philosophy by describing a method for arriving at clear and distinct ideas, arriving, that is, at certainty. The Cartesian method aims to unify science and philosophy by means of an exacting discipline of the mind in its approach to small steps of thought. It is in asking what exactly one and only one step of thought might be and how we might come to train ourselves to recognize the feeling of certainty as we complete each step that Descartes made a remarkable proposal in what we could call the psychology of discovery.

Second, in his treatise on the rainbow that was attached to his *Discourse on Method* he provided, as he wrote, a specimen or sample (*échantillon*) of that method. Descartes's solution to the mystery of the rainbow overthrew the Aristotelian account and gave him his one genuine experimental contribution to science. His remains the standard textbook explanation to this day of most of the rainbow's features. Descartes singled out the short work on the rainbow because, as he wrote to his correspondent Père Vatier, in all of the other treatises attached to the *Discourse* he had to follow a sequence for exposition that was different from the sequence of discovery.[5] Only with the rainbow was there a true specimen of the method itself.

Descartes's third Copernican revolution occurred in 1645 in his final published book, *Les passions de l'âme,* where he grandly announced that all other writers before him had reduced the soul to two primary passions, anger and desire, and that he would now reground the order and importance of the passions. What Descartes reacts against is a scheme of the passions as the scholastic tradition would have presented it. In Aquinas, for example, each of the twelve primary passions belongs to one of two groups, the irascible or the concupiscent; the template is either that of anger or of desire. The Scholastics themselves reach back to Plato in this and to the tradition of Stoicism. Plato had divided the soul into three parts: the intellect, the desires, and what he called the *thumos,* the angry or spirited part of the soul. The passions themselves make up, in all their variety, this third part of the soul, the *thumos,* and they are seen and imagined by means of what we could call the template of anger. The details of the passion of anger are taken as a paradigm or template.

Descartes's Copernican revolution within the passions rested on making wonder the first of the passions. In setting out its features he sets out a new template for the passions in general, and grounds human nature in its capacity for wonder rather than in its capacity for anger. From the time of Plato and Aristotle, through Roman Stoicism and early Christianity, and from there on to Scholasticism, the philosophy of the passions had taken either anger or fear as the central instance. Fear or anger became the template through which the question of how any experience of being in a state of passion could be defined and its mechanisms made clear. The history of descriptions of the soul depends on the relation of reason (Plato's first aspect of the soul) and desire (Plato's second aspect) to either anger (the Platonic tradition's third part) or to fear (the Stoic and Christian third, or passionate part). Before Descartes, philosophies of the soul, or human nature, could be divided into those reflecting the design of fear and those reflecting the quite different design of anger. In each case, fear or anger or wonder, an account of what it means, per se, to "have an experience" is implicated in the theory of the passions.

Descartes's three revolutions, wildly distinct in field, in importance, and in durability, are, when looked at closely, part of one revolution. The analysis of wonder in the book on the passions makes it clear that in its connection to learning and to science wonder is a key part of the process described in the *Discourse on Method*. The method is not a process of the intellect alone, but of the intellect, energized by wonder, rather than need, driven to consider objects brought to the attention of the intellect by the surprise of wonder. On the other side, in every one of Descartes's later writings on nature, the appeal within the actual presentation depends on the psychology of wonder and explanation. In Descartes's late work, *The Principles of Philosophy*, the third part treats the visible world, and in section after section he supplies his explanation for the phenomena of the earth, the moon, and the planets. Each of the final problems begins with the Latin phrase "Nec mirabimur"—"It should not be found wondrous that . . ." For example, it should not be found wondrous that the same side of the moon is always visible to us or that the planets around Jupiter move more quickly. Each is "nec mirabimus"; the phrase is used like a litany in every passage, "No one should be astonished that . . ." The language of wonder and its aftermath, explanation, pervades his writing on every aspect of empirical or speculative science.

What we now only read as a self-contained work, the *Discourse on Method*, was published by Descartes as the preface to a book containing three other works, *The Dioptics, The Meteors,* and *The Geometry.* The middle book, *Meteors,* takes up a number of phenomena that are striking, exceptional, or, as we might say, wondrous. A meteor, thunder, and the rainbow are classic instances of puzzling, dramatic, rare, and marvelous events or objects within nature. Each causes wonder, and the opening sentence of *Meteors* notes that "We naturally feel more wonder for those things above us, than for things at our own level." [6] This tiny aperçu within the psychology of wonder explains the domination of the phenomena of the sky in any work on wonder. The *Dioptics* begins by noting the new stars and new objects on earth that "these wondrous lenses" ("ces merveilleuses lunettes"), telescopes, microscopes, and mirrors, have discovered, a number far beyond the inventory of those known up to Descartes's time. [7] This is an essential fact. The great cosmological work of the seventeenth century occurred at a time when there was a large set of objects in the universe seen for the first time. Galileo, Newton, Descartes, and Kepler worked within the horizon of never-before-experienced facts. The newness that is part of the element of first-time experiences within wonder existed in a unique way because of advances in lenses that culminated in Galileo's telescope and a few years later in Newton's improved, reflecting telescope. Spinoza, the best-known philosopher among lens grinders of the seventeenth century, wrote in the decades after Descartes not only a small book on the rainbow, but also the most important modern work on the passions, his *Ethics.*

The experience of first sight does not have to be physical. Once Descartes had solved the refraction of light by means of his law of sines, he could take this mathematical "lens" and apply it to the problem of the rainbow and see the problem in a way never seen before. The technological production of newness—the moons of Jupiter that Galileo could show with his telescope—or the newer details within objects that had always been known, like the moon or sun, worked side by side with the newness produced by mathematical techniques, first among them, Descartes's own analytic geometry that fused algebraic equations in two unknowns with plane geometry. This was also a lens—"une lunette merveilleuse"—in which each problem appeared as though seen for the first time.

A privileged position for the first generation within science after any new technique is introduced is one consequence of the psychology of wonder within discovery. Descartes, Galileo, Huygens, and Newton were the first eyes within a world made new by a critical mass of advances in lenses, in the theory of light, and in the mathematical techniques of the limit and series within analytic geometry and the calculus. Descartes's first sentence on the rainbow makes this newness clear. "The rainbow is a wonder of nature so remarkable and its cause has been from all times sought with such curiosity by philosophers [les bons esprits] and so little known, that I could not have chosen anything more appropriate to demonstrate how, by the method that I use, one can arrive at knowledge that all those who have gone before us, have never reached."[8]

To understand how the aesthetics of wonder and the poetics of thought are two sides of the same coin, I will look first at Descartes's definition of wonder in the *Passions of the Soul*. Then in the next chapter I will show the operation of wonder in the steps of his method and to do this I will look back to Plato for a striking example of the same method. Then in the fourth chapter I will turn to the history of the explanation of the rainbow in its relation to both method and wonder.

Descartes's Definition of Wonder

As he begins to ask about the order and number of the passions in the second part of his book on the passions, Descartes arrives at the passion of wonder *(l'admiration)*. "Whenever the first encounter with an object surprises us, and we judge it to be new or very different from what we knew before or even what we had supposed it to be, we are caused to wonder at it and are astonished [étonnés] at it. And since this can occur before we know whether this object is useful to us or not, it seems to me that wonder is the first of all the passions." It is first because it occurs before we know whether it is useful or harmful and therefore whether we love it or hate it, whether we feel desire or aversion for it. Each of these four responses depends on knowing whether the object is useful, good for us, or the opposite, harmful for us and therefore to be avoided or hated. Wonder occurs first. Unlike such passions as love and hate, desire and aversion, which occur in pairs, wonder has no opposite as Descartes goes on to observe. "It has no opposite because, if the object that presents itself has nothing in it that surprises us, we are not stirred by it and we consider it dispassionately."

We could say that since wondering at the object is what causes us to pause and notice it, the opposite is not some other kind of experience of it, but the state of not having an experience at all. Spinoza, who disagreed entirely with Descartes about wonder, and thought it an unimportant state, described wonder as a kind of stunned response to an object. We wonder at an object when in its presence the novelty of its features does not remind us of anything else. The mind does not move from this to that, a motion which we call association in the phrase "the association of ideas." And since for Spinoza such motion is the essence of the mind itself, wonder is a kind of defective state of the mind, because in wonder the mind is not really itself—it is not in motion. Wonder has a natural opposite for Spinoza in contempt. In the passion of contempt the mind in the face of an object is so little held by its characteristics that at every moment it thinks of something else. Spinoza's pair of definitions of wonder and contempt in the third part of his *Ethics*, the one being the mind stalling in the presence of an object, breaking down, and the other, the mind in flight from it so that it never enters the association of thought which is the mind's chief activity, make clear the more encompassing and powerful definition of Descartes.

The idea of wonder is expanded by Descartes in a second definition: "Wonder is a sudden surprise of the soul that brings it about that the soul goes on to consider with attention the objects that seem rare and extraordinary to it." Its use to us is that it "makes us learn and retain in our memory things that until then we were ignorant of."[9] The passion leads us to apply our understanding, which our will engages in a particular attention and reflection. Those who lack a natural inclination to the passion of wonder are ordinarily very ignorant.

The capacity to feel wonder falls midway between two defective alternatives. First, a stupidity that never wonders because it never notices anything. Nothing strikes dull minds as interesting, genuinely fresh or new. This is the alternative of dullness. The second alternative is just the opposite: those who find everything amazing or striking, even the trivial differences of surface, monstrosity, oddness, and the merely strange. This addiction to marvels Descartes calls astonishment (*l'étonnement*—the French word is derived from the word for thunder, as our word thunderstruck is), and it is the distinction between astonishment and wonder that saves the second for intellectual, scientific uses. To be dumbfounded by miracles or tricks, the bizarre and the odd, is just as hostile to the process of wonder as the stupidity that finds nothing surprising. Astonishment is the pleasure we take in the face of the magician's tricks. It never leads to explanation or even to thought. Astonishment is a technique for the enjoyment of the state of not knowing how, or why.

In Descartes's time an essential part of the new science was the protection of the category of wonder (the rainbow, for example) from the concept of miracle. In a miracle God suspends the laws of nature to raise the dead, part the waters of a river, heal the blind. In a writer like Augustine a scientific wonder like the operation of the magnet stands side by side with the divine miracles. One reason that so many key works in the methodology of science have been either on the magnet (Bacon and Gilbert) or on the rainbow has been the part played by the methodological need to distinguish these phenomena from miracles and magic tricks. By Descartes's day the Protestant term "hocus pocus," which comes from the consecration of the Catholic mass, where the priest changes the bread into the body of Christ with the words "Hoc est corpus meum," had drawn a line against miracle and magic altogether. It was on the grave of magic tricks, religious miracles, and, especially, "Wonder-Cabinets"—those museums of prescientific confusion about wonder where two-headed calves, bleeding crucifixes, and scientifically interesting stones and magnets were jumbled together—that the new concept of Cartesian wonder was erected.

In addition to the alternatives of a dullness incapable of noticing the new and an astonishment that happens too commonly to be anything more than a confusion about the odd and the superficial, there remains a third alternative which Descartes does not consider. Hume and Hobbes, among many others, have claimed that fear is our fundamental response to suddenness and to the unexpected and the strange. Hume, for one, makes this claim in his section on the passions in his *Treatise of Human Nature,* writing that all unexpected or sudden experiences evoke either fear or a state of turbulence, motion from this to that in the mind, which we read as fear.[10] For Descartes, the pleasure and interest that we take in the rare and unusual is part of a purely intellectual curiosity that seeks to make sense of whatever is new within experience by means of understanding. Wonder, curiosity, and successful explanation notice the world and then renormalize that world, by fitting the exceptional back into the fabric of the ordinary.

In a world not yet sufficiently familiar, the predictable response to the extraordinary is a feeling of alarm that the novelty will turn out to be dangerous to the fragile order that maintains the self. Cartesian wonder is a middle state made possible by a history of confidence and familiarity, an overcoming of randomness by the installation of an ordinary world and the surpassing of fear by pleasure as the response to the unexpected. The state of wonder that leads to curiosity and investigation is the beginning of philosophy and the first of the passions, but, for Descartes, it is not the end.

Once the unexpected is questioned and found to be a varied form of the familiar, then wonder is over in this individual case. But just as wonder arises and leads to thought, and thought in its turn leads to an explanation that dispels wonder—as in the phrase "Oh, so *that's* what it is!"—so, too, in the larger frame of time the capacity to feel wonder, in general, is exhausted.

That the unusual leads to pleasure rather than fear must be based on our general success with explanation, our mastery of experience that lets us renormalize most situations. That we do not find ourselves for the most part defeated by the unusual, left baffled in an unresolvable way so that we "give up" and think of something else, provides the experiential base for the pleasure of the sudden, the unexpected, and the extraordinary. If each unprecedented thing should, in experience after experience of novelty, turn out to be life threatening, then fear would be the response to novelty that our actual experience itself would bear out and train us to feel. Similarly, if what struck us at first as unusual were to remain, for the most part, permanently baffling, then, once again, it would not be wonder but indifference that we would feel. Preferring not to be frustrated and have the weakness of our powers of explanation proved to us again and again, we would write off the novel as the uninteresting after a long training by experience.

The fact of wonder is, then, itself a profound experiential result. Against fear it is possible precisely because the novel is not usually threatening. Against indifference, wonder has survived because on the whole wonder is a technique of curiosity, interest, and attempted explanation that has often paid off in renormalizing the extraordinary, which we first react to by feeling wonder. In *Hamlet* the appearance of the Ghost of the dead king leads Horatio to say, "O day and night, but this is wondrous strange!" (1.5.164). The unexpected he calls by both its names: wondrous and strange. At the same time he reminds us of the ordinary and familiar: day and night. Hamlet answers him with a remarkable line that picks up Horatio's phrase "wondrous strange." He says, "And therefore as a stranger give it welcome." The moment of wonder or the appearance of a stranger is the classic opportunity for fear. Yet just as hospitality makes the stranger welcome and testifies to the empirical experience that on the whole this has not proved disastrous, so too the experience of wonder welcomes the strange as a stranger is welcomed. It too benefits from a history of experiences of too-frequent fear that in the end proved baseless. Wonder and hospitality, in Hamlet's phrase, rely on the harmlessness of the world, in most of the unexpected ways we find it.

Wonder is the hospitality of the mind or soul to newness, but only where the security of the self has already been secured so deeply that security, a feeling implying the reality of fear, but its suspension, can itself be forgotten. The privileged position of Descartes's generation within a truly new visual world of Galileo's telescope and Kepler's laws did not uniformly produce a renaissance of wonder, a unique situation for the acceleration of explanation and speculation. Although the balance between fear and pleasure in the face of the unknown is an empirical fact in that it depends on a history of intellectual success and an atmosphere of almost cosmic, as opposed to social, peace, that general balance does not translate, for every person living at a time or within a context of confidence in knowledge, into an interior balance of the same kind. In confident times there are still many apocalyptic thinkers, and within the general intellectual conditions of wonder that are among the powerful features of seventeenth-century science and philosophy, the exceptions can, from their side, make clear just what the structure of wonder itself was, but now by seeing it from the dark side of the same mirror.

Pascal's Alternative: Imagination, Terror, Abyss

Descartes's regrounding of the passions in wonder has, in the work of his near contemporary Pascal (d. 1670), its antiphonal voice. Pascal, whose greatness as a mathematician equals that of Descartes and whose scientific consciousness spans the years from Galileo to the early work of Newton, calls up the same experiences that in Descartes lead on to the aesthetics of wonder with its pleasure and then to explanation, but subjects those experiences to a religious capture that is unmistakably part of an aesthetics of fear. Pascal's single most often quoted saying contemplates the universe of Kepler, Galileo, and Newton, but with a newly intensified and justified fear: "Le silence éternel de ces espaces infinis m'effraie." ("The eternal silence of these infinite spaces fills me with dread.")[11] In Pascal, the word *effraie* with its active violence—to frighten, to terrify—works in a matrix with the Cartesian words for wonder *(l'admiration)*, marvels *(merveilles)*, and astonishment *(l'étonnement)*. The very things that in Descartes would fall into one or another of these two categories of wonder or astonishment with their opposite intellectual and moral consequences shift in Pascal into this more important third term, the terrifying. What Descartes calls a wonder, Pascal will often call an abyss ("une abîme").

In Pascal's longest and most stunning picture of the human condition he places man between two infinities, the infinitely large scale of the universe, in the face of which man is insignificant, and the infinitely small, in the face of which he is a monster. Each of these two infinities would usually call up a catalogue of wonders, of pleasures, of astonishments, but for Pascal, each is an abyss. In his invocation of the minute, Pascal seems at first to be leading toward an encomium—the rhetoric of wonder—but by prolonging and extending the contemplation he leans us over his abyss. In his evocation all the key words are present for his aesthetics of terror.

> But, to offer him another prodigy [prodige] equally astounding [étonnant], let him look into the tiniest things he knows. Let a mite show him in its minute body incomparably more minute parts, legs with joints, veins in the legs, blood in the veins, humours in the blood, drops in the humours, vapours in the drops: let him divide these things still further until he has exhausted his powers of imagination, and let the last thing he comes down to now be the subject of our discourse. He will think perhaps that this is the ultimate of minuteness in nature.
>
> I want to show him a new abyss [abîme]. I want to depict to him not only the visible universe, but all the conceivable immensity of nature enclosed in this miniature atom. Let him see there an infinity of universes, each with its firmament, its planets, its earth, in the same proportion as in the visible world, and on the earth animals, and finally mites, in which he will find again the same results as in the first; and finding the same thing yet again in the others without end or respite, he will be lost in such wonders [ces merveilles], as astounding [étonnantes] in their minuteness as others in their amplitude. For who will not marvel [qui n'admirera] that our body, a moment ago imperceptible in a universe, itself imperceptible in the bosom of the whole, should now be a colossus [une collosse], a world, or rather a whole, compared to the nothingness [néant] beyond our reach? Anyone who considers himself in this way will be terrified at himself [s'effraiera de soi-même], and, seeing his mass as given him by nature, supporting him between these two abysses [ces deux abîmes] of infinity and nothingness, will tremble at these marvels [ces merveilles].[12]

Pascal's images are meant to pulverize that classically proud boast of humanism: man is the measure of all things. Man is the creature who, terrified of his measure when set within the measures of nature, becomes, in the end, terrified not of nature, but of himself, the creature between two abysses. Within Pascal's thought we pass subtly from the seen to the imagined, from the visual to the imaginary extended by simple extrapolation. The mite's leg, bloodstream, and humors are all potentially visible, but what follows is only imagined, and it is the imagination rather than sight—that locus of wonder for Descartes— that swamps the world of the visible by sinking it into the endless extension that the imagination proposes to the visible. Pascal is anti-scientific to the extent that the imaginary comes to give its tone to the visible rather than the visible giving its tone to the imaginary. The blood circulating in the leg of the mite is a tender image, not a terrifying one. It is only the dizzying vortex of worlds within worlds that can later capture and efface our first tender response to the actual scene.

Pascal makes clear the path by which the very discoveries of the new science could be reabsorbed back into the religious sensibility and used against themselves, and he does so by casually using the visible as just one short segment of inner vision, that is, of what we can imagine.

Pascal's is an abyss of lenses. The new microscope of Leeuwenhoek and the new telescope of Galileo reawaken a theological horror of the infinities they reveal, which, instead of exhilaration and curiosity, unleash profound depression and terror. Only the geology of the nineteenth century in combination with Darwinian thought, which set man within an infinity of time and development, could have added a third insult to Pascalian nature equal to the telescope and the microscope. But here, too, Pascal slips from the physical to the imaginary. Geological time, for example, asks us to set our history within some millions of years and not the 6,000 years of the Biblical story, but these millions of years are not infinity at all. In fact the exact time of cosmology is decisive in understanding the size of the universe. The microscope revealed ever smaller mites, bacteria, and finally viruses and proteins, but it did not reveal infinite regress, worlds within worlds, in a dizzy spiral. The scales of the universe were suddenly expanded, but Pascal willfully merges the very large into the infinite, the very small into a second infinite, then calls each an abyss.

The words of Descartes, *l'admiration* and *l'étonnant*, are, by using the same technique, sunk within a framework of human powerlessness and insignificance. The very appeal of wonder to human powers of discovery and pleasure in being able to contemplate the marvelous are, in Pascal, neutralized or tainted by the more powerful theological vocabulary. Each infinity turns itself into an abyss. Each subject of wonder, like the blood in the mite's leg, falls into an infinite regression of a dizzy and almost nauseating kind. The marvelous gives up and puts on the black suit of the terrifying.

In Pascal the last stand of the contemplative aesthetics of fear takes place within the mathematical and scientific new world of the seventeenth century itself, not opposite it in the contemplation of demons or the eternal fires of hell, those more familiar topics of theological terror. What kind of an aesthetics does Pascal set in front of us? The crowding together of extremities is well known as a central device of Baroque art, as is the use of the infinite. In the Baroque aesthetics of strong effects, the lightest and the darkest sections of a work are crowded next to each other, while vast spaces are implied between things. Round domes or ceilings are painted to seem to disappear into skies and infinite regress. Pascal's image and Baroque aesthetics are two elements within the Counter Reformation's terrorism directed at the new scientific spirit.

In Pascal, Baroque aesthetics joins forces with the Inquisition to set up an inner reign of terror (man *terrified at himself* in Pascal's stunning phrase) to re-humble man and win him back for a spiritual life of fear. Descartes's dismissal of fear in his book on the passions is equal in importance to his vision that the alternative to wonder is anger (the irascible). Descartes calls fear "a coldness . . . a perturbation and astonishment [étonnement] of the soul, which takes from it the power of resisting the evils which it thinks lie at hand."[13] The coldness is the opposite not only of the warmth of delight and wonder but of the very different heat of anger. That Descartes calls fear an astonishment takes account of the fact that, like wonder, fear is linked to sudden and surprising experiences. Here we see the deeper reason for his repudiation of astonishment *(l'étonnement)*. It is not just that astonishment is an excitement in the superficial differences, the odd and the monstrous, and that it has no drive toward questioning and learning. More profoundly, it is astonishment's deep connection to fear and to a conception of human nature grounded in fear that sets it at the opposite moral pole from wonder in Descartes's thought.

Pascal, whose primary word is always astonishment rather than wonder, works through the same materials as Kepler, Descartes, and Newton. Harvey's masterpiece on the circulation of the blood stands behind Pascal's vision of the blood in the mite's leg. Pascal reshapes these materials to deform their psychological consequences. In Pascal, a whole century's excitement at being the first human beings to look through microscopes and telescopes (a thrill clearly felt in those passages in the work of Pascal's equally religious contemporary, the Puritan John Milton, when he describes in *Paradise Lost* looking through Galileo's telescope) chills to depression and to a feeling of insignificance and human frailty. This frailty is the preparatory step to a total surrender of the spirit to religious discipline, to biblical truth, and to reliance purely on God. It is a only a prelude to the collapse and then surrender that led Pascal, after a mystical experience that took place, he notes almost like a laboratory scientist, between 10:30 and 12:30 on the night of November 23, 1654, to his entry into the disciplined Jansenist community of Port Royal and his "renunciation totale et douce," his total and sweet renunciation, and his "soumission totale à Jésus Christ et à mon directeur," his "total submission to Jesus Christ and to my spiritual director."[14] The Pascalian is not an alternative comportment of the self but a step on the way to its collapse and the sweetness of its abolition.

Alongside the strongest version of the intellectual design of fear, as an alternative to Cartesian wonder, in the atmosphere of the new scientific world of the telescope and the microscope, this contrast between Descartes and Pascal brings into a new importance what we might call the protective side of the visual within thought. Pascal's turn depends on sliding from the visual to the imagined, by means of repetition and extrapolation without end. Mechanical repetition and extension are two of the essential poetic features of the thought structures of paranoia and obsession, those two mad versions of an intellectual science driven by fear. The imagination is a projective power, operating in just those realms where nothing is known or can be known.

Wonder is a response to the visible world. If we insist that the main locus of thought is the visible world, the part played by the projective imagination disappears. Aesthetics and the scientific (or Cartesian) use of the passion of wonder within experiences of the extraordinary unite in sheltering themselves within what we can now see as the protection of the visible. The imaginary, as we meet it in Pascal, although it seems to flourish within the same materials and even overlaps at first with the same range of feelings (the astonishing, the marvelous, the wonderful), differs fundamentally in ways that we can see by noticing that the imaginary has nothing to do with the extraordinary. The imaginary is quite simply free of the whole lawful play between the ordinary and the extraordinary. To put it even more strongly, the imaginary is also in its nature all that can never be experienced. The imaginary, like the Wittgensteinian ordinary, but in the opposite direction, is exactly all that is not experience. The two realms of the ordinary and the imaginary define from opposite sides of negation just what our notion of having an experience is about and how that experience is connected with noticing something or wondering at it.

With this point I circle back to the essential definition of wonder with which I began: a sudden experience of an extraordinary object that produces delight. Descartes places wonder first among the passions because it is the origin of intellectual life. To notice a phenomenon, to pause in thought before it, and to link it by explanation into the fabric of the ordinary: this is the essence of science in the widest meaning of the term.

Wonder Fades with Age

After this contrast to Pascal's terror, one final aspect of Cartesian wonder needs to be emphasized, at least in part, because it leads in its own way to a deep problem with and limit to the use of wonder. In each of its appearances wonder is temporary. Furthermore, it is most likely to appear toward the beginning of a discipline like optics or philosophy or, in the life of an individual, toward the beginning of intellectual life, or of thought in a given direction or upon a given problem. These many features have to be called the decay of wonder. They are not peripheral facts but, rather, essential to any accurate definition of its nature. Wonder is what we could call our best first chance within thought. Wonder makes up part of what we might call the youth of experience or thought. For the individual, too, the moments in which seeing occurs encased in wonder form a threshold or make up an initiation into knowledge that fades or becomes ever more difficult to recapture once familiarity has given an apparent inevitability to all things. Descartes describes the decline of wonder with care equal to that lavished on his account of its nature.

> And although this passion seems to diminish with use, because the more we meet with rare things which we wonder at, the more we accustom ourselves to cease to wonder at them, and to think that all those which may afterwards present themselves are common, still, when it is excessive, and causes us to arrest our attention solely on the first image of the objects which are presented, without acquiring any other knowledge of them, it leaves behind a custom which disposes the soul in the same way to pause over all the other objects which present themselves, provided that they appear to it to be ever so little new. And this is what causes the continuance of the malady of those who suffer from a blind curiosity—that is, who seek out things that are rare solely to wonder at them, and not for the purpose of really knowing them: for little by little they become so given over to wonder, that things of no importance are no less capable of arresting their attention than those whose investigation is more useful.[15]

In the remarkable opening of this passage Descartes makes it clear that not only must the contents of the experience be new, but the experience itself must be. It is not just that the rainbow must be as an object new to us, but that having this experience of novelty, pleasure, and excitement itself must be new. Once we become familiar with what the experience itself feels like—no matter what its content—the process of decline within wonder is already under way.

True wonder is a phase of the alert mind, of the mind in its process of learning. It wears out with age, situated as it must be between a dumbness unable to notice the extraordinary and a blind curiosity addicted to even trivial differences that can be experienced as "wonders" without leading to reflection or the pursuit of knowledge.

THREE

Wonder and the Steps of Thought

The Template of Wonder: To Be Human Is to Learn

The claims made for wonder in Descartes's analysis mark out an epoch in the description of human nature. He sets wonder first because it is by means of wonder that man learns. To profit from wonder man cannot be either inattentive or passive, since in these cases he would not notice differences, nor can he feel himself to be living in a world that is fragmented, anarchic, and unpredictable. The premise of wonder is that we live in a lawful world, one in which the laws of nature, no less than the extraordinary or singular events that seem at first exceptions to the laws and regularity of nature, provide pleasure. The experiential world in which wonder takes place cannot be made up of unordered, singular patches of experience. We wonder at that which is a momentary surprise within a pattern that we feel confident that we know. It is *extra* ordinary, the unexpected. For there to be anything that can be called "unexpected" there must first be the expected. In other words, years or even centuries of intellectual work must already have taken place in a certain direction before there can be a reality that is viewed as ordinary and expected. Only this makes possible the rare and privileged moment, against a normative frame, when the *extra* ordinary can take place and evoke wonder. This is what we mean by the difficulty of seeing, in the sense of noticing, the everyday, the customary, the obvious. This is the intellectual or scientific "ordinary" which makes up a second layer over and above the everyday world described by Wittgenstein in the earlier example of an ordinary shoe. Wonder is the middle condition between an unawakened intellect and a systematic knowledge so complete that there no longer exists anything unexpected.

We can now see that Descartes has displaced anger and desire as the first of the passions because, like Aristotle, he defines man as a being whose first delight is knowledge. The opening words of Aristotle's *Metaphysics* express this by means of one of the great tributes to the pleasures of the senses.

> All men by nature desire to know. An indication of this is the delight we take in our senses; for even apart from their usefulness they are loved for themselves; and above all others the sense of sight. For not only with a view to action, but even when we are not going to do anything, we prefer seeing (one might say) to everything else. The reason is that this, most of all the senses, makes us know and brings to light many differences between things.[1]

Descartes preserves this distinction between use and pure delight in knowing by claiming that it is the passion of wonder that distinguishes man from all other living things. Animals act and even think, but they do so in the light of interests that draw them toward the objects of their interests (in desire) and away from the objects hostile to their interests (in aversion). Wonder, which occurs outside and prior to any knowledge about whether the object falls within the realm of desire or aversion, marks off human experience as differentiated by a phase that is not superior to interest—not disinterested—but prior in time to interest. This is the second meaning of saying that wonder is the *first* of the passions.

Descartes's wonder has, like Plato's anger and spirit, a natural affinity to youth with its confidence and freshness. Youth is inevitably the stage of life in which even essential and prominent experiences are novel. The mistaken prolonging of wonder that Descartes calls blind curiosity, resting as it does in that trivial or marginal novelty of surface that is a constant feature of reality, amounts to the attempt of middle age to retain what was one of the natural features of youth. Stoicism, whose very premise is the unique accuracy of the account of life provided by maturity, and in particular the account provided by the emotional life of successful, but beleaguered, late-middle age, responded as antagonistically to wonder as it had to anger and grief. One of the best known of Stoic phrases is the phrase of Horace: "nil admirari" ("nothing is to be wondered at"). There is nothing new under the sun; a familiar and relentless natural order explains all that has occurred, is occurring, or will ever occur from the beginning to the end of time. Stoicism in its battle against the passions insisted on the reality of repetition within experience, thus ruling out unique or "first" experiences. At the same time it invented a training that amounted to a kind of practice that would prepare us so that, in effect, there could never be a sudden experience, a moment of surprise, a moment of the unexpected. Stoicism could be called a training in expectation. In Stoicism a highly accurate psychology of the passions can be read out by negation. "Nil admirari"—"Admire nothing!"—stands as the first commandment of that psychology.

Socrates' phrase "Philosophy begins in wonder" and Descartes's proposal that wonder be considered the first of the passions, because it is the very mechanism of an interest in differences upon which all learning depends, imply that human speculation and creativity, because of their link to wonder, are finite, declining as age increases, and linked to first experiences and, therefore, to youth. It is a decisive piece of evidence for their claims about wonder that most great discoveries in mathematics and science are made by scientists in the first years of their careers. The breakthroughs occur in the minds of those closest to the point in their own intellectual lives when the central facts of the discipline have the freshness that can strike the mind with wonder. Many problems in mathematics, unsolved for generations and to which other mathematicians have given years or decades of thought, are solved by fresh minds whose major advantage is that none of the details of the situation are covered over with familiarity so that a division into the obvious and the strange has taken place. In the same way, the sudden shift of a discipline to a fresh set of questions as a result of a single discovery frequently makes possible a cluster of discoveries because, for a brief and rapidly declining moment, all observers are made "young" in this new territory. The capacity of mathematics to state the same thing in an almost unlimited variety of alternative forms, argues for the need to continually look at the same as though it were entirely new.

The scientific pathos of the liquidation of wonder by explanation runs like a thread through Descartes's work. His book with its many warnings against blind curiosity or astonishment—those false twins of wonder—expresses caution about and even fear of wonder in its everyday forms. He was not alone in recognizing this paradox of the passionate side of discovery that in driving us to learn, drives us to find ourselves back within a slightly expanded ordinary world. In *The Science of Mechanics* the philosopher Ernst Mach discusses the motto that was used by Stevinus in 1605 on the title page of his text in mechanics, which was printed in Leyden thirty years before Descartes's *Discours de la méthode* was printed in the same city. The motto in Dutch reads "Wonder en is gheen wonder." Mach comments: "As a fact, every enlightening progress made in science is accompanied with a certain feeling of disillusionment. We discover that that which appeared wonderful to us is no more wonderful than other things which we know instinctively and regard as self-evident; nay, that the contrary would be much more wonderful; that everywhere the same fact expresses itself. Our puzzle turns out then to be a puzzle no more; it vanishes into nothingness, and takes its place among the shadows of history." [2]

Stevinus sets as his motto the paradox that wonder is the enemy of wonder. Like Descartes and Mach, he loops together the beginning and the end of the string of thought, the "Ah!" of wonder and the "Oh, so *that's* what it is!" of successful explanation, where the word *that* reminds us that to explain is to recognize something that we already know underneath the apparently extraordinary. Explanation re-normalizes temporary or apparently extra-ordinary anomalies, bringing them back into the ordinary world.

The pathos comes from leaving out the middle, or the process of thought itself, to contemplate only the moment of fixing on a problem, and the final moment of solution. Also left out is the question of whether there ever is a final moment of complete explanation. With Descartes and earlier with Plato, it is precisely in this middle that the method of science meets and thrives by means of the charge of wonder. We notice by means of an experience of wonder brought on by the sudden, unexpected appearance of an object; but within the process of thought it is against the background of frustration and of effort in directions that have proven fruitless, against the errors that are the real point of "trial and error," that the surprise of finally "getting it" takes place.

One and Only One Step

The first major work of Descartes was his *Regulae*, or *Rules for the Direction of the Intellect,* and in this manual where he worked out the rules for the orderly and secure work of the mind we can see a clear relation to the later description of wonder in his final published work. What the rules seek to do is to create a situation where only one step of the problem stands before the mind, isolated from all irrelevant details and distinct as a step from any earlier or later steps of the same chain of reasoning. Descartes wants to make it possible, as in a chess game, to have only a single move to make. Just as in a chess game, he also wants to design a way to make sure that every necessary fact is visually present to the mind at the moment when this next step is being weighed and that, as in chess, pieces that have been made inactive have been removed from sight. On the chessboard, the player's glance can take in every piece, its position and its possibilities. At the same time, nothing is on the board that is not part of the situation at the moment, that is, the game itself.

Many of Descartes's rules are designed to create, for the mind in the process of thinking, exactly this drama of thought: one and only one move, the presence before the mind of every relevant fact, and the elimination of every irrelevant detail. For Descartes a key means to this chessboard situation is the use of diagrams and the use of algebraic symbolism. In the diagram every detail is present to the eye at once. What is eliminated is the use of memory within thought, replaced by a deep use of the visual. Descartes mistrusts the memory as a place to store all the facts that we need for this one step of thought because one or another might drop out of the mind at a crucial moment. But even more, if the memory is used, the mind also has to keep reviewing. In passing one by one over the facts stored in the memory, it distracts itself from looking at the single, carefully articulated gap that it has to leap.

The diagram or equation brings the simultaneity of the visual sense into play and suppresses the memory. This was, as we saw in the very beginning of the discussion of wonder, one of the key details of wonder. Here again there is a certain antagonism to memory because it involves both repetition and recognition. In the religious story of Noah, the flood, and the rainbow, we saw designed into experience a distraction by the memory that calls up a story or explanation at exactly the aesthetic moment of wonder. Cartesian science builds in this either/or of memory and wonder in insisting on the crowded, simultaneous space of a diagram or equation over against reliance on the movement between memory and thinking that all work without diagrams involves. Within the diagram the details are pressed as close together as possible, almost as though they were already solved.

The diagram implies that we think best with only a single sheet of paper in front of us. This is the scientific style of blackboard thinking in the modern world. But how does a diagram or equation articulate exactly the state of the problem up to this step or gap where we now find ourselves?

Descartes himself, in the *Rules*, uses a problem applying the Pythagorean theorem to demonstrate how symbolic notation isolates one and only one step within a process of thought.[3] We usually think of the Pythagorean theorem in its overall form: $c^2 = a^2 + b^2$, which expresses visually the whole process, but no individual step within it; the square of the hypotenuse is equal to the sum of the squares of the other two sides. The equation makes possible a number of facts or problems: $a^2 = c^2 - b^2$ or $b = \sqrt{(c^2 - a^2)}$ as well as several others, each of which would define one problem in the family of problems possible in the more encompassing equation. It is important to notice that the general form in which we remember the equation—$c^2 = a^2 +$

b^2—is a form that does not define any goal that we would usually be trying to reach. We would almost never be trying to learn c^2.

Descartes's diagram defines the visual situation at the outset of the problem in which all that is known is represented, along with what remains unknown. A parsimony of symbols requires that we do not label or invent references for details of the drawing that are not under consideration; for example, a letter d to represent the sum of the two sides a and b, or an angle ø to represent the angle between sides a and b. These facts exist, but the problem does not concern them. The essence of symbolism (algebra) consists in symbols referring to actual discrete entities within the problem, and that there be no more symbols than the problem requires. Here is the literal meaning of Descartes's larger program of clear and distinct ideas. The diagram for the problem of finding the length of the third side c is shown in Figure 3.1.

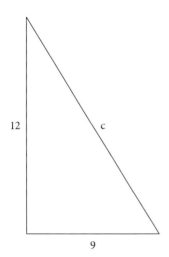

12

c

Figure 3.1 Finding the length of the third side *c.*

9

Within the act of thinking itself it is neither this diagram of the problem as a whole nor the general formula that is important: each is a summary, or reminder of the general case. In using the Pythagorean theorem to find the length of the third side of a triangle whose first and second sides are of length 9 and 12, Descartes observes that a mathematician would write √(225), meaning that what must be found, the length of the third side, is the square root of the number gotten by adding together the squares of the other two sides. Obviously, this is not the first step. In fact, it is the next to the last one. It is, however, a statement of one and only one step of the problem because only one operation—that of taking a square root—is proposed. The formulaic element $\sqrt{225}$ is an instruction to take that step and the number is given on which the operation will take place. Many earlier steps have already taken place, such as squaring the number 9, squaring the number 12, and then adding together the two results (81 and 144) to get the number 225, on which the next operation will take place. Each step has its own representative diagram or equation in which only the act to be done next is made visible. Each representation is a highly charged moment of instruction. In this case the steps would be:

1. a

2. a^2

3. b

4. b^2

5. $a^2 + b^2$

6. $\sqrt{(a^2 + b^2)}$

The two versions of the equation, $c^2 = a^2 + b^2$ and $c = \sqrt{(a^2 + b^2)}$, actually describe two different steps or moments within the process of thought. Descartes points out that to see step number 6 clearly the equation should be written $\sqrt{(81 + 144)}$ and not $\sqrt{(225)}$. The second equation fails to keep distinct for the mind the actual things represented. The number 81 represents the square of 9 or, geometrically, the square with a side 9. The number 144 represents the square of 12 in the same way. But the number 225 actually represents nothing at this point; it cannot be attached to any part of the diagram. As the sum of two squares, it is not anything literal within the terms of the problem. Not only must a diagram represent a single moment of the action of thought, but it must also preserve the distinct parts and use no symbols that fail to refer to a distinct part. At the moment after adding $a^2 + b^2$ we do not use an arbitrary letter k to represent this quantity so as to say, now take the square root of that sum (which I am calling for convenience k). We cannot write the step as $\sqrt{(k)}$. But this is just what we seem to be doing in writing $\sqrt{(225)}$, because both k and 225 are transitional composites that have no reference in the problem itself. We could not put our letter k anywhere on the diagram. The diagram keeps symbolism honest in inventing only the minimal number of algebraic symbols—a, b, c in this case—and in controlling our own awareness of those moments when something has been created in the process of thought that no longer refers. Thus the step must be represented algebraically as $\sqrt{(a^2 + b^2)}$.

What is Descartes trying to isolate by means of these rules in which symbolism and, above all, the force of visual simultaneity take over to control what we know to be a temporal problem—the steps of a proof? What we are looking at here in this simple case is the motivation behind Descartes's greatest accomplishment, his analytic geometry, which brought algebraic equations into geometric, visual representation by means of what we still today call Cartesian coordinates, the graphing system for solving equations with more than one unknown.

By means of the interplay between symbolism and the visual, Descartes breaks down any complex problem into just those steps that can be resolved in a single intuitive moment of seeing. Each one leads to a moment of exclamation: "There!" or "Ah!" or "Now I see it!" The intuition is clear, distinct, and certain. The rules, diagrams, and equations set the stage for the simplicity and confidence of this instantaneous act of "seeing." We complete the step and move on to arrange the next one. Each step of thought has the potential to leave us stalled in front of it saying, "I can't get it!" "I don't see what happens." "I can't see it." This experience of duration, of not getting it, is the background to the sudden moment of saying, "I get it!"

Each of these moments is a moment of wonder—a pure experience of one and only one new thing. And this experience of wonder occurs as the aftermath of the duration within which we say, "I just can't see it!" Often at the moment of getting it, we smile. Each of the passions has its own instantaneous physical act—the tears of grief, the red face of anger, the pallor or trembling of fear. Of these, it is the smile of wonder that often appears on the faces of the Greek statues of the gods.

For Descartes, a diagram clears away the clutter of details in order to bring out the structure of those that remain so that this and only this one thing stands ready for thought. What is important for Descartes in traditional Euclidean geometry and in arithmetic is that these are the only disciplines that had ever become clear about just what constituted one and only one step. If we look at a proof in Euclid and see that it has 16 steps, we might ask: Why aren't there 7 steps or 91? Why is a step just this much and not smaller or larger? In philosophy this question had never been solved, although the medieval use of the syllogism was one attempt to achieve a solution. In the dialogues of Plato, Socratic conversation is also an attempt to isolate, by means of the question-and-answer style, this problem of one and only one step of thought. Only in mathematical proof had the unmistakable clarity about what constituted a complete and yet distinct step of thought been secured. It is for this reason that both Newton's *Principia* and Spinoza's *Ethics* were written in the form of geometric proofs.

Descartes recommends practicing thought by going over small problems like this one of the third side of a triangle so as to learn to recognize the feeling of certainty. Even though we are not actually doing any new thinking in solving a problem within a formula that already exists for the general case, we can observe in a unique way within these already given problems the fact of what one step looks like, what adequate symbolism is at any moment, what the distinction between relevant and irrelevant details feels like, but above all, what the feeling of "getting it," of crossing the small gap of the unknown, is like. We can watch ourselves learn in this small controlled repetition of thought. This is the meaning of Cartesian certainty and its link to clear and distinct ideas.

So far we have seen what we could call a "wonder-like" experience in the small steps of the proof, as Descartes has set it up by his method. Because we move around in what is already known, there is no true example of discovery here. In science or mathematics each new person, doing a problem that is new to him or to her, is recreating the moment at which the first person saw this relation. Wonder is a relative fact. It concerns what is new to me, what is my first experience of a Chinese landscape painting, or of a mathematical proof, or of playing through the moves of a chess masterpiece. This is one reason why the kind of practice that Descartes suggests lets us at least recognize discovery and certainty when we do reach them ourselves. Plato in the dialogue *Meno* set out to show actual discovery itself, a moment of learning which is also a moment of wonder. By looking carefully at this example we can see the full meaning of the poetics of thought, much of which is now clear as a result of this analysis of Descartes.

Plato's Meno *and Learning by Wonder*

In Descartes, we follow a set of steps that have the disadvantage that every step goes in the right direction. The proof is unalloyed progress. As a result we see no representation at all of trial and error, which we know to make up a decisive part in learning and discovery. By contrast, in Plato's *Meno*, we find before us precisely the process of making mistakes as parts of the search for an answer, mixed with confusion, false starts, and backtracking, all of which prepare for the moment of being "lost in wonder" that makes the answer a flash of discovery. The Platonic wondering is also a wandering—an erring— that more accurately represents the process of thinking than the display which Descartes acknowledges to be a perfect exercise in which we practice a psychology that we will have to learn to apply later elsewhere.

The pages of the *Meno* in which Socrates elicits from an untaught boy the proof of a complex and unexpected theorem in geometry are the best demonstration that we have of the process of reasoning and learning. By the end of the demonstration the boy knows one clear thing that he did not know before, or, to use Plato's vocabulary, one thing that he did not know that he knew before. He also knows how to do something. In this case knowing something is less important than knowing how to do a certain procedure. Furthermore, once the boy has learned how to double the area of a square he has also learned how to teach this to anyone else. He has not learned a formula, but has participated in a discovery that puts him in possession of the full internal logic of what it is that he knows and just what the order of the steps must be. In terms of the distinction Descartes made about his own work on the rainbow, the order of discovery and the order of exposition are the same.

At the heart of this short instance of learning is a moment of wonder composed of intellectual surprise, the unexpected and the pleasurable. It is also a moment that once again depends on the power of the visual—a diagram—to make possible, because of the simultaneity of many details before the eyes and mind, a flash of insight that yields the solution. Because the learning that we see in the *Meno* is a discovery, it is also a model for thought in general. Descartes's example of applying an already known general case—such as the Pythagorean theorem—to a local instance can never be a model for open-ended thought.

Socrates sets in front of the boy a diagram of a square. Each side has a length of 2. The area of the square is therefore 4. The question is: How can the area be doubled? How can we get from this square to a second square with an area of 8? The structure of the problem is significant. There is an explicit question to which an answer must be found. We have in front of us all the elements of the question—a square, the length of the sides that composes it, the notion of doubling. Only by working with and transposing these already given elements will the answer appear. Because diagrams play a key part in thinking within Socrates' example and within the aesthetics of thought, I will reproduce the diagram for each stage of the process. First we have the known square, shown in Figure 3.2.

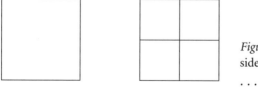

Square side 2   Area 4

Figure 3.2 Square with the side of 2 and the area of 4.

The boy's first attempts will exploit the most obvious line of thought. Since we want to double the area, we must double the length of the side. He tries the answer "4." When we draw the new square we find that it has an area of 16, not 8 (Figure 3.3). The first try was an error, but a rational error, quite different from a guess of "7" or "613," mere random numbers that would show that the boy wasn't thinking at all.

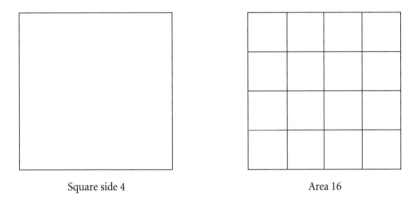

Square side 4   Area 16

Figure 3.3   Square with the side of 4 and the area of 16.

By comparing his new area of 16 to the desired goal of 8, the boy sees that he has overshot the mark, but in a very significant way. He has gone exactly twice as far as he wanted. His first mistake preserves the "doubling" arrangement, but he doubled the answer rather than the area. His second answer is, then, with great intelligence, "3." Since his first answer took him twice as far as he wanted to go, he now thinks that if he goes halfway between 2 and 4, he will end up halfway between the areas of 4 and 16. His guess of 3 gives a third square, now with an area of 9 (see Figure 3.4).

After his first wrong answer he did not turn back to the starting point, erasing the mistake from the page or from his mind. The error itself exists and is part of the material of the problem as he now sees it. His solution will, in the end, be the outcome of his history of errors. Even more important, he cannot unthink. His relation to the

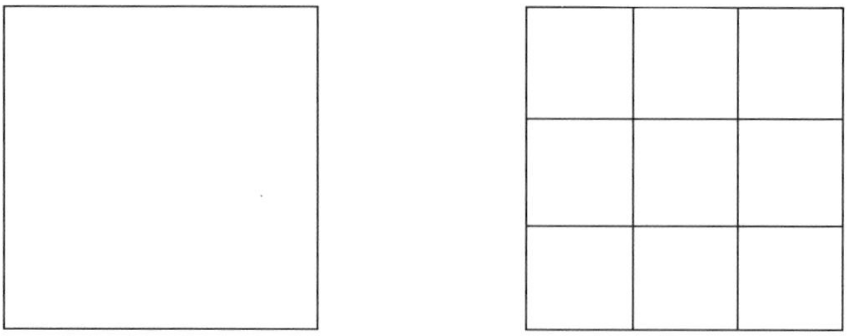

Square side 3

Area 9

Figure 3.4 Square with the side of 3 and the area of 9.

problem is no longer an innocent one. Now he has this error to carry around with him. He looks at the wrong answer, comparing it to the answer he wants, and cleverly chooses halfway between.

Now the boy has reached perplexity. In Socratic terms the boy now, at last, knows that he does not know. This helplessness is also part of the process. He has exhausted every obvious, reasonable step in terms of the given words and in terms of what he already knows. But now Socrates returns to the first mistake—the square of 16 that is twice as large as we want. He superimposes the first square, with a side of 2, and we see that we have four of these squares (Figure 3.5).

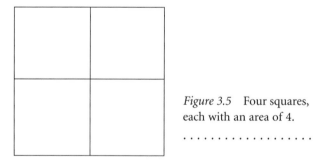

Figure 3.5 Four squares, each with an area of 4.

Now he asks the decisive question: How might we get half of this square that would still be a square? If we drew a line across the middle we would have half, that is an area of 8, but it would be a rectangle (see Figure 3.6). If we drew a line from corner to corner it would be

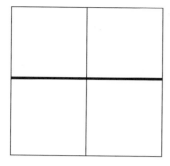

Figure 3.6
Two rectangular areas of 8.

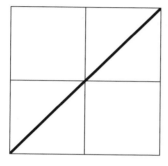

Figure 3.7
Two triangular areas of 8.

an area of 8, but it would be a triangle (see Figure 3.7). Socrates then draws the line that solves the problem. He draws the diagonals of each of the four little squares (see Figure 3.8).

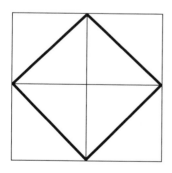

Figure 3.8
One square with an area of 8.

Almost by miracle we find, tilted on its side, the square which must be half of the area of the whole because it is half of the first small square, plus half of the second, plus half of the third, plus half of the fourth. This ingenious repicturing of the problem is the moment of wonder. Instead of seeking to double something, the boy finds half of something. He reverses the problem. At the same time, he rotates the square in space. All earlier trials had kept the lines vertical and horizontal. It is important to notice that it was in making the first mistake that the boy gave us this square that was too large, but that mistake led, once we contemplated it a certain way, to the solution to the problem. The mistake had to be made.

Next, the ingenuity or cleverness of the unexpected solution also arises out of a persistent set of trials and errors with the question of how to cut the large square in half. The second answer, the diagonal line that gave us two triangles, actually only needed to be used in an unexpected way to get the new square. Within these trials and errors we see that after a certain amount of time we have put in play many things that were never in the original diagram—the diagonal line or lines, the square made up of smaller squares. The solution upsets the mental categories with which we began. We were trying to find something larger than the first square, but could only do it by finding something smaller than a square that was never given in the statement of the problem. The two areas of 4 and 8 can only be connected by means of a third, imaginary area of 16, which was never included in the statement of the problem, but to which the first two areas are both in a clear relation even while always remaining in an obscure relation to each other.

The problem, we might say, is solved by sinking both the problem and the solution into a third thing of which they are each a part. This submerged relation is clear in the final diagram. The surprise and unexpected direction of the solution—the rotation of the square, 45 degrees from where we expected to see it; the fact that the solution was found in the relation "one half" rather than in the relation "double" with which we began; and the fact that it was the process of finding out that one was wrong (creating the square of 16) while not letting go of the error: these are the components that constitute a remarkable miniature version of thought itself, the poetics of thought. All poetics involves making an artifact. Here it is the imaginary object—the artifact of the square of 16, divided in four by small squares with their diagonals, divided in fact into eight triangles, four of which also happen to make up the needed square—that is the invented or made thing within the problem.

The moment of wonder is only important in that it takes place within and by means of a process that can be stated as a sequence of precise single steps of thought, a series of attempts, distinct acts of construction, in which each time one new thing is done. At each moment it is clear just why one would do this step next, why this would be the next attempt. At each moment we could say out loud—as Socrates does in the dialogue—"Isn't it obvious that . . . Now, isn't it true that . . ." The answer each time is, "Yes." The proof is plodding, dogged, and mechanical while being, at the same time, ingenious, imaginative, and wonderful. The interconnection between these two seemingly opposite series of qualities describes the relation of science to wonder, and it makes clear the passionate energies that are inextricable from exacting thought.

The design of question and answer in the Socratic method is the first and probably the best attempt in philosophy to take over from geometry and science the Euclidean proof in which exposition and discovery follow the same path and in which the questions put to someone who does not know make certain at every moment that he has taken the last step with certainty. If he were not certain he would raise objections or announce his confusion. By saying "yes" to each question, he controls the thinking of Socrates so that only one step is taken at a time, and, equally important, the passage to the next step always goes by an obvious route. If the route is not self-evident, then a step has been left out. The order and the atomization of the argument into single steps make up, when taken together, the relation of certainty to surprise which is the relation of wonder.

In Plato's small drama of learning, the tension that builds up in the mind of the student is made up of perplexity and, to some extent, frustration. Both follow on the recognition that "I don't know," which is, here, reduced to the statement "I don't know what to try next." Knowing that one does not know is a classic step, in the Socratic method, on the way to knowing, and to being certain of what one knows.

The psychological states of being perplexed and frustrated are not accidental within thinking. They are often prolonged and agonizing, as anyone who has ever taught geometry knows. We say over and over, "I can't get it!" or "I just don't see it!" We trace and retrace the steps, hunting for a way out, but we find ourselves back at one of the many dead ends. The details of the problem disintegrate into a set of facts that seem to have no real connection to one another: just the opposite feeling to that of the "fit" of a solution. We come to doubt that we have all the facts, or to think that we have failed to discard certain details that keep taking up time but lead nowhere.

In all of this time, which can last for hours, the tension and frustration mount. In fact, there might be no solution. The situation might be impossible. The paths of the problem take on the feeling of a labyrinth that leads again and again to a dead end. Then unexpectedly, and in a second of time, the answer strikes us. The pieces assemble into a tight, interconnected condition where everything fits.

The experience of exhilaration in the moment of solution is in some direct way related to the perplexity and to the disintegration of certainty and direction that preceded it. Perplexity is the mental state of being "lost." At this point it is clear what Theaetetus' state of being "lost in wonder" was about. One of the basic feelings as you face an unsolved geometry problem of this kind is that you are immobilized in front of it. It doesn't go away, and you can't make any progress. Such immobility defines part of the feeling of freedom in the moment of wonder, a moment when we suddenly race ahead, cover all the distance to the solution in an instant. The normal reaction at the moment of solution is to race back through step after step, seeing each for the first time as certain and right.

The relation of frustration to this moment of discovery points to the deep inner plausibility of Plato's theory that we never learn anything at all. Rather we have forgotten it, and in learning something we remember knowledge that we have always had. What is intriguing here is just how similar the experience of being stalled in front of a problem is to the situation where we are trying to remember a name that we know we know but cannot think of. The pressure on ourselves to remember it, the tension and frustration, feels nearly identical to the experience of working at a geometry problem that we can't get.

Since the problem is one that we have never done before, we cannot (in our sense of the word) already know it. But in working to remember a name we strain and concentrate and then, suddenly, by surprise, it "leaps into the mind." The suddenness of its arrival, the pleasure and relaxation of tension in remembering, has the same structure of feeling as the sequence for solving a problem. This is the acute and telling side of Plato's theory that knowing and remembering are closely related. This psychological similarity does not depend at all on believing the theory that we have lived many earlier lives— the theory that Plato uses to explain the similarity between the experience of learning and the experience of memory.

The moment of seeing a solution for the first time is the quintessential intellectual experience of wonder. The exclamation "Aha!" or, as we always say for Archimedes, "Eureka!" which we now refer to by the nearly technical term of "Aha-erlebnisse," contains the passionate moment of learning itself. Plato, like many later thinkers, took geometrical reasoning as the model for all thought for two reasons: first, because the exact chain of proof could be exhaustively stated in a rigorous manner; and second, because the experience of the novice in looking at each new step, once all previous ones are felt to be certain, is the experience of "Aha, now I see it!" Each step recreates the experience of wonder and then the transformation of wonder into certainty. One important feature of Plato's proof in the *Meno* that all learning is a form of remembering depends on the experience of surprise and pleasure that is expressed in the "Aha!" experience. If we picture the moment of confusion in any problem or reasoning just before we "see" the answer, we realize that that prior state is psychologically identical to the state in which we are trying to remember something that we are certain that we know, but cannot for a moment remember, such as the name of a street on which we lived twenty years earlier. Suddenly, the name appears in the mind and the release of the tension of trying to remember occurs and we say, "I've got it!" The state of tension as we look at a figure in geometry and try to get the next step of the proof, and then suddenly "see" the next step, saying "I've got it!" is so strikingly similar to the act of remembering something that Plato's argument, carried out by means of a geometric proof in the

Meno, that all learning is remembering becomes at least psychologically plausible. The process of Socratic dialogue is designed to reason by means of a verbal equivalent to the step-by-step sequence of moments of "seeing" that something must be so. Both Newton and Spinoza wrote using the geometrical method because, in addition to the large-scale rigor of the method, the step-by-step process builds in the experience, for the reader, of the act of discovery that occurred earlier for the scientist or philosopher, and that sequence of small-scale acts of "seeing" is, precisely, the sequence of wonder.

In Socrates' demonstration, the moment of learning one new thing is isolated before us along with the experience of suddenness and surprise that makes up the pleasure of the moment of learning. The relation of being lost in wonder to the moment of intellectual wonder itself is also clear within Socrates' example, since, the darkest hour (after the failure of the second attempt, the proposal of a length of 3) is, in terms of the Baroque aesthetics of crowding dark and light together, right next to the moment of illumination. One final puzzle about these few pages within the *Meno* will force us to turn Socrates' demonstration itself in a surprising direction, like the square that Socrates rotates 45 degrees after he has had us considering only upright, standing squares for the whole time of thinking about the problem.

Socratic Silence

If we return to the original question that Socrates asks, we might notice that he asks only how we would double the area of the square. The original square has sides of length 2. Why does Socrates not ask just how long the side of the new square will be? Once we reach the end of the problem we do not know this length. It is passed over in silence. Naturally, it is not necessary to know it, since the one and only question was how to construct a square double the area of a given square. Yet every one of the boy's attempts at an answer involved a guess about the length of the side of the new square—4 or 3. Why does this question of the length disappear from the problem?

What drops into silence here is the fact that the side has no rational length; it cannot be measured. It can be expressed by an irrational number, two times the square root of 2, but the square root of 2 cannot be expressed by any fraction. Earlier in Greek geometry it was the very scandal of this irrational number √2, which is the outcome of trying to compute the length of the diagonal of a square with a side of length 1 by means of the Pythagorean theorem, that led to the crisis within Pythagorean mathematics, a crisis connected to its mysticism and to its secrecy. According to legend the discoverer of this problem was put to death. He had, at the very heart of the rational, reached the irrational.

The example that Socrates has chosen here is one where geometry parts company with measurement, or with arithmetic. To construct the square is a geometric solution, one that yields complete satisfaction, but it is a solution that does not depend on knowing any of the lengths, or even on assigning a length in the first place. The given square can be exactly doubled with a compass and straight edge, not necessarily a ruler—the straight edge need have no markings and can be of any length. To measure the length is impossible. No ruler of any size will yield a whole-number answer for its length: this is the meaning of saying that it cannot be expressed as a fraction. The denominator of the fraction is the length of the ruler; the numerator is the whole-number measure in terms of that ruler. This mysterious fact remains hidden within Socrates' proof at just that moment when we stop talking about numbers (after the failure of the guess of "3").

But even this is not the whole meaning of the irrationality of this expression. Both Aristotle and Euclid give elegant proofs to demonstrate that when we ask about the length of the diagonal of a square whose four sides each measure 1, the number that would solve this problem would have to be both odd and even. It would have to be divisible by 2 (even) and not divisible by 2 (odd). It is not only unmeasurable but ruled out by logic itself, the law that the same thing cannot both be and not be something—in this case, divided by 2. Since this law is fundamental to the act of thinking, this number cannot be thought about. And yet the problem of this number turned up in no remote corner of mathematics but in the simple question of the length of the diagonal of a square each of whose sides is 1.

If we set aside the problem of logic for a moment (odd and even at once), the irrational length "the square root of 2" is not a subject of wonder because it is in Socrates' time irrational, a threat to mathematics itself which will have to be, just like Socrates' own pair of squares, built into a more encompassing structure before it can be a candidate for wonder, that is, for surprise and then explanation.

Wonder is a feature of the middle distance of explanation, outside the ordinary, short of the irrational or unsolvable. What falls into this far distance of the irrational, the unsolvable and the unthinkable, can, in time, move into the horizon of wonder or even into the core of the ordinary. Wonder is both personally and historically a movable line between what is so well known that it seems commonplace and what is too far out in the sea of truth even to have been sighted except as something unmentionable. This moving line, as it changes from period to period, lights up our interest and passion for explanation. It attracts us to itself. It is the horizon of the ordinary and the everyday which is constantly changing its location. The feeling of wonder, when and where it surprises us, notifies us of just where that boundary is at the moment. This we could call the part played by wonder in drawing us to the zone of unsolved but solvable questions.

Socrates does not ask the question "How long must the side be to double the area of a square made up of sides with a length of 2?" Within the mathematics of his day this is not a question. The expression "twice the square root of 2" can be given an approximate answer: 2.2832. . . . But the dots that trail off into an infinite decimal tell us that the answer is approximate. We can say the answer is "2" or "2.3" or "2.28" or "2.283" and so on. The answer is not correct, but varies depending on how exact you need to be at the moment.

The disappointment when we hear this type of answer—"Well, it depends on what you need"—shows why the question is asked in the way that it is and why Socrates constructs his demonstration of rational thought on the basis of a problem that had hidden within it the very irrational itself. It is this movable line of wonder that also makes up our capacity to distinguish what is a question or problem at any moment and what is not. The irrational itself is only relative and represents, like wonder itself, a certain horizon of the moment. In this case the word *irrational* shows the collapse of the requirement that we be able to measure—that is, to create a ratio between two things. Arithmetic and algebra can use the expression "twice the square root of 2" within calculations without falling into the logical abyss brought about by any attempt to say what the square root of 2 finally is. Only the requirement of a ratio, the problem generated by the physical act of measurement, is permanently impossible, thus making the number "irrational." Nonetheless, the famous statement of modern mathematics—God made the integers, the rest was made by man—finds in Socrates' silence a tacit nod of agreement.

Socrates' silence, once we violate it by bringing up the very thing that his discretion conceals, tilts his problem 45 degrees. But now we can see that the design of the question is a key component of being able to answer it at all. One question—"How long must the side be of a square twice the area of this given square?"—would lead to an abyss of thought. The other question—"Can you construct a square exactly double the area of this given square?"—skates over this very abyss because it uses but never brings up certain things. The very water in which thought would drown is frozen over to let the skater pass.

It is a remarkable fact about the saying "Philosophy begins in wonder" that in the dialogue *Theaetetus,* shortly before Theaetetus spoke of himself as lost in wonder, he had mentioned in passing exactly this problem of squares of area 3 or 5 or 8, the squares that had led to the proof of the irrationality of the expression the square root of 2. Just as in the *Meno,* the problem itself is passed over in silence. Aristotle was the first, in his *Posterior Analytics* 1.23, to jump on the ice itself and break through to demonstrate that the number is a logical impossibility. What is clearly known within the silence of Plato and Socrates is at last spoken by Aristotle and then Euclid.

But in the Socratic silence what becomes clear is that the poetics of thought depends on a negotiation around certain topics as well as a direct engagement with others or with other versions of the same problem, as in this case. The moving line of wonder is the mechanism of this engagement with some but not with other problems. Socratic silence is one side of the coin of a poetics of thought.

Explanation and Demystification

By tracing out the scientific claims for wonder in Descartes's book on the passions and then using examples from Descartes and Plato to show the small-scale meaning of the experience of wonder within thought, I have now reached the point where both the aesthetic side of wonder and the scientific side are before us. The aesthetics of wonder seemed at first to limit itself to our first instant of being struck by an object within nature. We say that in wonder the object calls out to us, making a claim on our attention. Built into this idea of a first instant is the fact that wonder must trail off as the experience progresses. Unlike desire, whose climax of intensity occurs near the end, just before satisfaction, wonder like each of the primary passions—fear, anger, and mourning—has its peak of intensity in the first moments and then declines or complicates itself.

What does wonder change itself into if it does not simply fade? Descartes's answer is that it leads to the search for explanation; or as Socrates said, it leads to philosophy. Within the idea of reasoning that we see in Descartes and Socrates, wonder continues to play a part in the moment-by-moment experience of intuition. Within the frame of a well-designed local question, we suddenly "get it." The suddenness, surprise, unexpectedness of direction, as well as the pleasure in the outcome, which when taken together make up the psychological elements of this experience, repeat, but now in an intellectual-aesthetic form, the very features of the first experience of wonder itself.

This series of later experiences of wonder have to do with the fact that scientific explanation is not in search of *the* secret or *the* mystery of the rainbow. The idea of a single point of explanation is fundamental to the religious or mythological style where there is one story— God, Noah, the flood, the covenant—that completely and finally settles the question as a whole. The connection of wonder to scientific explanation follows from two things. First, the experience of wonder involves our turn from the experience as a whole to the contemplation of its details. Since explanation drives us to produce as many details as possible that fit within the explanation, the number of separate experiences and points of explanation is potentially very large. Each can be a separate step of thought, a distinct experience of "Now I see why that is so!" Second, the experience of wonder also occurs repeatedly and in surprising directions because, as we saw in the problem of the two squares from the *Meno*, the solution often comes by inserting the problem into a wider frame than was initially given, within an artifact that has come into existence during the process of thought itself. Or, the explanation is seen at a moment of restating the terms in equivalent but imaginatively different symbols that have their own built-in paths of thought. In combination these two details of explanation lead to an unpredictable number of turns and surprises within any explanation and to the fact that every explanation will be not one answer but a series of details, each of which fits what we can notice within the original experience once we have attended to it closely. Cartesian wonder is what makes us interested in this and not that, and it is what binds us to it long enough to discover its nature in detail.

Why does the description of discovery not limit itself to the first person who solves a given problem or who takes a step of thought and even, in his or her case, to the first day on which the act of seeing takes place? As we read through a proof like that in the *Meno* we experience the same surprise, suddenness, and unexpected direction within the solution to the question. Even though we have not ourselves discovered it for the world, we have discovered it for ourselves. Since it is new to us it takes effect in the moment as though it were new per se. Wonder is a horizon-effect of the known, the unknown, and the unknowable. It is like the rainbow itself, relative to where you stand, and is produced uniquely for each person. Unlike the rainbow it occurs at different times as well as in relation to different things. It is a highly personal border of intelligibility; the place where at this moment in our own history and development we are able to see a question. The place where we are able to say "I wonder . . ." Discovery only adds to this the almost accidental fact that no one has ever stood in this place before, wondered about this, and given an explanation.

With this link between the first aesthetic call of wonder and the intellectual process of disciplined thought with its own spatialized, instantaneous features, we have reached the point of facing a final stage. In Descartes we can recognize both a celebration of the passion of wonder and a deep suspicion of it. When he warns against blind curiosity or distinguishes wonder from astonishment, we sense a nervousness about how easily "real" wonder can be confused with these dangerous counterfeits. In the connection of wonder to youth we have almost a built-in tragedy for intellectual life as a whole, which like life in general is made up of a brief youth and a long aftermath of youth. If discoveries can best be made between the ages of sixteen and thirty, what does the life of thought from thirty to seventy amount to? How can one live in the aftermath of one's own best powers, like the Olympic athlete retired at twenty-four? This would be less important if wonder were only one of many techniques of thought and aesthetic delight. If it is the primary one, then we are left with Descartes's dilemma: either a life made up of superficial attempts to hold onto the now lost feeling of wonder—blind curiosity—or a kind of lifetime elegiac relation to our own lost powers. Within poetry this elegiac self-relation describes exactly the central topic of Wordsworth's greatest poetry, written in celebration of feelings and powers that he once had, but now no longer finds within himself.

These suspicions of wonder are personal and psychological. In Descartes's larger picture, explanation seems to dispel wonder, by the very act of fitting the extra-ordinary and the singular into the web of ordinary things. In Spinoza's vocabulary, once something is explained we think about it by moving from it to other things that it now reminds us of. Singularity is the opposite of the commonalty implied when anything reminds us of something else. Once explained, the object enters our ordinary processes of association. The path to explanation leads us back to the ordinary world, where we now discover that whatever we had wondered at and found extra-ordinary now has its place. Thinking seems to be part of what Max Weber called the demystification *(Entzauberung)* of the world. Paradoxically, Weber, whose description of modern rationality as the demystification of the world is one of our most fundamental clichés about the modern period, is describing the very same modern period—roughly since Copernicus and Kepler—that Descartes characterized when he set wonder as the first of the passions, opening up a description of the new scientific age as an age in which we identify human nature with its capacity to learn by means of wonder. Descartes's idea of modernity is the modernity of scientific wonder, and this same modernity is Weber's demystified world. Can Descartes's separation between wonder and astonishment solve this paradox? Does Weber refer only to an end of mythological explanation, the end of the age of miracles, as even the Church had acknowledged? Is wonder, in the Cartesian sense, secured as a concept only once we have separated it clearly from the idea of a local exception to the laws of nature (the miracle) or from explanation by genesis rather than cause (the rainbow's genesis is God's act of putting it in the sky on a certain day and explaining why he was doing it)?

Max Weber's term *Entzauberung* is a composite word formed on *Zauber* or magic. The strife and overlap between this cluster of terms—wonder, magic, astonishment, miracle, monster—marks out a turning point in modern times, and like all turning points it is not a point at all but a long zone of time in which confusion among these terms, deception or exploitation of the overlap among them, was one of the open resources of thought on the way to a modern conception of science. The monstrous, for example, can seem to be part of the wondrous—a two-headed calf—but the confusion between the slight nausea that we feel in the face of the monstrous and its special way of being extraordinary, its mixture of fear and curiosity, its failure to elicit or to lead to thought, are all distinct from wonder. The monstrous gives greatest pleasure to the anarchists within philosophy because it seems to imply that there are no laws, only averages or habits. Wonder is the pleasure of the lawful mind, and it is distinct from the pornography of fear that plays its part in the monstrous.

Weber's theory can be shown to be in harmony with Descartes's because they both are ruling out the miraculous and the astonishing, but at the same time we can see in Weber, but not in Descartes, a dispassionate idea of rationality and thinking itself that is one strain in modernity, a strain opposite to the Cartesian stress on the part played, not by emotion or feeling, but by passion within thought. Because Weber seems allied to Descartes's own suspicion of certain aspects of wonder, the challenge of this picture of the outcome of explanation has to be examined. Can wonder be the passion that lures us into a process that would end up by squeezing out the passions altogether? In *The Passions and the Interests* the economist Albert O. Hirschman has argued exactly this about the part played by avarice within modern capitalist society since the seventeenth century.[4] Hirschman sees that certain features of the single passion of avarice— its need for regularity and predictability within the future, for example—actually set it at war with the features of the passions in general. By using avarice against the passions as a whole, we pass from a culture of the passions to a culture where each man or woman is defined by his or her interests. Could the same be said of wonder? What is the final state of the process? To this point I have looked at only the beginning—the first instant of wonder—and the middle point of the steps of thought.

To look at this end point of explanation itself I need to return to actual experience. The weakness of the example of the triangle problem in Descartes and of the doubled square in Plato's *Meno* lies in the fact that however much wonder we might experience in the process of thinking about them, they are not themselves objects of sensory wonder. Our reason for thinking about them in the first place was not an experience of wonder in which the object strikes us, calls attention to itself and leads us to wonder about it.

The triangles and squares of geometry do not exist in ordinary life. In contemplating them or solving problems concerning them, we work with the mind's own symbolic artifacts, not with the sensory world. Although the visual plays a part in the diagrams of mathematical demonstration, the visual itself is an altogether different experience, one in which, for example, the visual field is always crowded. To attend to the rainbow we do so against the claims of trees or cows. The line of the hilltop, the flowers near our feet also are part of the same visual field at a certain moment.

It is only within genuinely aesthetic experience that this hinge where wonder holds together thought and perception can be realized. And it is only here that the question about the loss of wonder through explanation, the *Entzauberung* of the world—if these two should turn out to be related—can be solved. One way to ask this question is to ask if we are not using a false idea of explanation that involves a final moment when every question has disappeared. Is there explanation at all in any complete and final sense? Or are we here reimposing the wrong idea of the "secret" or the "mystery" that will be dispelled with explanation, the magician's trick that once we know his secret will interest us no longer?

Historically, from Aristotle to the nineteenth century the science of the rainbow has turned out to be just this hinge where wonder holds together aesthetic perception, with its pleasure, and thought, with its distinct process and pleasure. As one historian of science has written, "the explanation of the colors of the rainbow had been from the beginning associated with the whole problem of the nature of light and its propagation in a homogeneous medium and at the interface between two media."[5]

Aristotle and Descartes represent the two epochal moments within the science of the rainbow, but at least some of the questions surrounding the rainbow will remain open so long as light itself has no persuasive, final inventory of features and master explanation. That we still find ourselves in the twentieth century with the intellectual awkwardness of needing both a wave and a particle theory of light is, like the presence of the odd *and* even number in the background of Socrates' proof, a clue that here, too, the part played by a strategy of silence will be essential. One of the most intriguing questions in any long history of explanation is just how compensations were built in so as to, as we might say, freeze over the false components of the explanation as well as the abysses of thought so that thought itself can skate over and continue on its way. Until Newton showed that white light could be separated out into the spectrum of colors and that those colors could then be reassembled into white, all earlier work on the rainbow had used false theories of color. How thought proceeds successfully, immunized against the false and unknowable features that it is forced to carry within the explanation itself, is one of the elements of a poetics of thought.

FOUR

Explanation and the Aesthetics of the Rainbow

Fear of Explanation and Explanation by Fear

Wonder drives out wonder. This motto of Stevinus links the suspicions of Descartes to the convictions of Romantic poetry two hundred years later. Wordsworth's lines "My heart leaps up when I behold / A rainbow in the sky" capture in the emphatic three words "heart leaps up" the poetics of wonder set within a moment of passion. The heart is the physical organ that is metonymic for passion in modernity, as the *thumos* was for Plato. He called the *thumos* the rushing and boiling part of the soul. The *thumos* in Homer and Plato is the site of anger understood as a template for the soul entire; the heart is the site of the modern passion of love—which since Spinoza and Rousseau has been our template not only for the passions but for inner experience itself. The heart localizes, as the *thumos* had earlier, the fact that there is a physical component of the passions, the blush of shame, the trembling of fear, the tensed muscles of anger, the smile of wonder.

The leap that Wordsworth gives as the heart's action lets us see behind the metonymic image of the heart a second figure, that of a youth. More accurately we would say that the heart races; and historically, running had been one major image of the passionate state.

We find it in Plato as well as in Homer's *Iliad,* where Achilles was known as the great runner. But for the heart to leap up, we must half-see the second image not of a running man, but of a leaping youth. Wordsworth's full poem seems to trail off, as Descartes said that wonder itself does, but here into stale resolution, emphatically repeated three times:

> My heart leaps up when I behold
> A rainbow in the sky:
> So was it when my life began;
> So is it now I am a man;
> So be it when I shall grow old,
> Or let me die![1]

The pair of lines "A rainbow in the sky" and "Or let me die!" are set parallel in the stanza and they are emphatically linked by the rhyme— sky-die. The exclamation mark that we expect earlier as the sign of wonder occurs after the word "die" instead and implies the determination of a man taking a vow (So be it!) rather than the ejaculation of wonder (A rainbow!). The fade-off into prose of the three mechanical lines (So was it . . . So is it . . . So be it . . .) has in its declining energy something of the depression of aging itself. We almost have here Hegel's conflict between the poetry of the heart and the prose of the world, but now as stages of individual life. Wordsworth resolves that this split must not happen, but his need to pledge himself with so much exaggeration ("Or let me die!") proves that he knows it will happen or that it already has.

In the famous dinner of December 28, 1817, Wordsworth joined a group of poets to drink to Newton's health and to "confusion to mathematics." John Keats, who had been present along with Wordsworth, wrote a short time later the lines in his poem *Lamia* that are one of the best-known expressions of a split between poetry and science. The lines are also examples of what Max Weber saw as the essence of modernity, the disenchantment of the world, its rationalization that results in *Entzauberung.* It is important to remember that Weber writes as a sociologist and not as a historian of science. His rationalization is the rationalization of social life and politics; its natural form is bureaucratization, the shift of power from individuals to structures, from charismatic to systematic leadership. Weber writes not of our relation to sun and stars, but of our relation to taxation and the Prussian civil service.

Keats had earlier passed through medical training, and many doctors know of the changed relation to the beauty of the body as a result of study, especially dissection, that might be taken as a perfect example of Weber's *Entzauberung*. The demystification of the body as a result of medical knowledge is, I hope to show, an outcome entirely different from the consequences of the analysis of light in philosophy and mathematics. Every stage of explanation starting with Aristotle and Euclid and on to Newton, and from then to the present with its lasers and quantum effects, has consistently dispelled the extraordinary only to produce, in the very act of explanation, newer forms of wonder and newer experiences of wonder within those very things that were now, at least in part, explained. The inventions on the way to the explanation of the rainbow were themselves a catalogue of wonders.

Keats's often-quoted lines have convinced readers of poetry for almost two hundred years of a necessary warfare between scientific thought and poetics and, more especially, between the coldness of scientific perception and a now lost passionate relation to the visual world. One reason to recollect the part played by wonder in initiating knowledge, as well as the close relation between the steps of thought and the process of poetic wonder, is to show that a poetics of thought would push to the margins the antipoetic idea of science that always has as its other side an anti-intellectual idea of poetry. Keats's lines from *Lamia* speak of the outcome of explanation rather than the process of discovery.

> Do not all charms fly
> At the mere touch of cold philosophy?
> There was an awful rainbow once in heaven:
> We know her woof, her texture; she is given
> In the dull catalogue of common things.
> Philosophy will clip an Angel's wings,
> Conquer all mysteries by rule and line,
> Empty the haunted air, and gnomed mine—
> Unweave a rainbow.[2]

In Keats's phrase "an awful rainbow" we have his word for wonder: inspiring awe. That the rainbow is always referred to as she in these lines imbeds the description in an already emotional and humanized world of love poetry. In its later history, the word "awful" has declined almost further than Keats's rainbow itself, to mean bad or, in slang, lousy. "How bad was the movie?" The emphatic answer is "Awful!"

For Keats the word still implied religious reverence and wonder, but with an element of fear rather than delight. An elegiac mood or one of regret for the loss of a richer past makes up the pathos of this type of thinking within modernity, where the sky is described as once filled with mythological figures and angels. The picture is contemplated and used in the same way that the now long-gone agricultural way of life and the knowable community of small towns are aggressively used as nostalgic indictments of empty modern life. Keats goes on to speak of the sky as "emptied" by knowledge. The choice between fullness and emptiness asks us to regard modernity as a pure state of negativity, a history of losses.

The very revealing word "charms" that Keats uses to describe just what cold philosophy has driven from the world shows, in its gentility and love of the decorative, an incapacity—not present at all in Wordsworth—to rise to the full experience of the rainbow in the first place. Keats also draws his line between charms and the "dull catalogue of common things" that results once we come to knowledge. Philosophy, he goes on to say, will "Empty the haunted air . . . Unweave a rainbow"—in short, "Conquer all mysteries by rule and line." Keats's word for the air before science is a revealing one, like the earlier word "charms." He speaks of it as "haunted" and of science coming to "empty" the air. Thirty years later in the *Communist Manifesto* Marx would begin with the words "A spectre is haunting Europe," and he too wrote of an apocalyptic advent—in his case, not science but revolution.

Like Keats's use of "awful" instead of "wondrous," his use of "haunted" shows that he is speaking of a world of mystery that is in part a world of fear. He gives us almost a detective story or Gothic mystery version of science. Knowledge empties the sky of its ghosts. Keats's own poetic catalogue in these lines shows us what he means by a catalogue that is not dull or ordinary and intends to point us to the richer, better world prior to philosophy. He surrounds the rainbow with charms, mysteries, angels, and gnomes in mines. From this poetic catalogue the rainbow passes to the "dull catalogue of common things." For Keats the rainbow is similar not to thunder, snow, and the stars, but to gnomes and angels; nor does he interest himself in the quite different ways that we have lost contact with imaginary creatures like gnomes in mines or trolls under bridges and, on the other hand, with real sensory objects like rainbows. The rainbow continues to exist for our senses and for our experience, but with knowledge added. The angels and gnomes cease to exist as a result of that same knowledge.

The gnomes in mines can be thought of as a personification of our feelings of fear and mystery as we go down into a mine. The same is true for our uncanny feeling about the dark areas under bridges, a fear and danger that figuratively names itself "trolls." I have expanded Keats's words to bring out the part played by fear in his template for any passionate relation to the world. Because science has changed the ratio between human power and nature, science has had a profound effect on the prevalence of the experience of fear in everyday life. The simple example of lighting at night makes this clear. If our template of the passions is a template of fear, then it will be true that the diminution of fear that is one of the key achievements of civilization, of peaceful social arrangements, of science, and of the technological conquest of nature will seem to have been paid for by a loss of a passionate relation to the world. Fear and science are hostile, but is the same equation true of wonder?

If wonder is the template and not fear, is there any diminution of our passionate connection to nature if what has been diminished is only fear? More important: Is wonder in the same either-or relation to knowledge as is fear? Does science or knowledge empty a sky of wonder as it might empty a sky of fear once we have lightning rods, shelter from storms, and knowledge of the harmlessness of comets? Astronomy, in replacing astrology, has emptied the sky of a world of signs and meanings that were mostly omens. The lightning rod put an end to a whole genre of sermons that explained to the congregation just what evil had been brought to light by the lightning striking just this particular church or that farmer's barn. Lightning had been taken as a sign, just as the rainbow was in the story of Noah, but after explanation and Ben Franklin's lightning rod, it was "emptied" of fear and of the kind of narrative sense that fear and suspicion could raise about every strike of lightning as a sign from God. If these sermons had been true in the past, then wasn't the installation of a lightning rod an interference with God's intention to strike just this tree, that barn, this steeple as a punishment or warning? And since steeples had often been the highest point in the landscape, did the higher number of strikes on churches mean that God specifically used lightning to point out the sins of parishes by striking this church and not that one?

Was the sky emptied of its charms once the Protestant pastors of Europe no longer gave Sunday sermons explaining the family sins or the parish sins that were revealed by the lightning strike and fire? If a passionate relation to nature is above all understood as a relation whose features can best be seen in an experience of fear, then the consequences of explanation for passion per se are clear. The deeper question also appears: Why do certain times or philosophies comprehend passion per se through a paradigm of anger or wonder, fear or grief?

Fear and wonder are equally possible, alternative responses to the sudden and to the unknown. Hume and Hobbes, along with the earlier Stoic philosophers, made of fear the fundamental relation to experience. For Hobbes, society exists because of mutual fear. The possibility of wonder is itself an unexpected fact since the intuitively more obvious response to the unknown would be fear. Wonder depends on an empirical run of experience in which the strange has, in the end, not turned out to be harmful. Similarly, the pleasure of seeking explanations has to reflect a general success in finding answers. If there were only a long human history of frustration and defeat when explanation was attempted, the habit of posing questions would go out of style, replaced by an ironic or an anarchistic relation to the events around us. Both wonder and explanation are evidence for a long history of empirical success and therefore pleasure in the novel, the sudden, and the as-yet unexplained within our culture.

In most early societies the rainbow was seen either through an aperture of fear or through the almost opposite aperture of wonder. Folk beliefs have claimed that at the ends of the rainbow there were either pots of gold or a promise of disaster for any hut or barn the ends seemed to rest on. So great was the Peruvians' fear of the rainbow that they believed one had to stand in silence until it disappeared. Many societies believed it was dangerous to point at a rainbow. In at least one culture it was claimed that a person who crossed under a rainbow changed sex.[3] Like the pot of gold at the end of the rainbow, this change of sex plays on the subtle fact that since the rainbow is like our shadow, we can never reach it. Whenever we advance toward it, it moves farther on. We cannot cross under it for the same reason. The pot of gold and the change of sex remain utopian possibilities.

The Dull Catalogue of Common Things: Genus, or Explanation by Kind

Keats does not list just what makes up his own idea of a dull catalogue of common things. So we can supply our own out of philosophy's history of interest in the ordinary and the everyday. We can use Wittgenstein's shoe from the discussion in the *Brown Notebook* and Heidegger's hammer from the section on tools in *Being and Time* and the remarkable piece of wax that Descartes used as his example of an ordinary thing in his *Meditations*. Shoe, hammer, and piece of wax point us in the direction of the everyday as something that we can pick up with our hand, but each of the three is also an example of an object filled with human meanings and uses, an object made by man—a manufactured object as we could say, part of the human poesis of making and using.

Only in Surrealism could the rainbow be set alongside the piece of wax, the shoe, and the hammer. Aristotle set it in a very different catalogue in his logic when he used it as an example of how we classify, making the brilliant point that echoes, rainbows, and reflections in mirrors were part of the same genus. To join sound and light in this way shows a profound grasp of the structure of the instances, a structure that was not mathematically clear until the work of James Maxwell in the nineteenth century. To group rainbows and reflections led Aristotle to speak of two different kinds of mirrors, one that returned images and a second, weaker mirror that returned only colors but no image. Aristotle's list set the rare and ungraspable rainbow among the more common, indoor experiences of an echo or one's image in a mirror.

In the thirteenth century Robert Grosseteste (1168–1253) wrote a book on the rainbow that began an outburst of European speculation parallel to the equally rich Arab work. Roger Bacon (1219–1292), continuing Grosseteste's work, listed a more concrete and realistic set of instances of rainbows, and he spoke using the language of experiment rather than that of classification.

> And further let him observe rowers, and in the drops falling from the raised oars he finds the same colours when the solar rays penetrate drops of this kind. The same phenomenon is seen in water falling from the wheels of a mill; and likewise when one sees on a summer's morning the drops of dew on the grass in a meadow or field, he will observe the colours. Likewise when it is raining, if he stands in a dark place, and the rays beyond it pass through the falling rain, the colors will appear in the shadow nearby; and frequently at night colours appear round a candle. Moreover, if a man in summer, when he rises from sleep and has his eyes only partly open, suddenly looks at a hole through which a ray of the sun enters, he will see colors. Moreover, if seated out of the sun he holds his cap beyond his eyes, he will see colours; and similarly if he closes an eye the same thing happens in the shade of his eyebrows; and again the same phenomenon appears through a glass vessel filled with water and placed in the sun's rays. Or similarly if someone having water in his mouth sprinkles it vigorously into the rays and stands at the side of the rays. So, too, if rays in the required position pass through an oil lamp hanging in the air so that the light falls on the surface of the oil, colors will be produced. Thus in an infinite number of ways colours of this kind appear, which the diligent experimenter knows how to discover.[4]

Here in what Bacon reports as the work of diligence and experimentation we can see a catalogue of the everyday that is anything but dull or commonplace. The rainbows around mill wheels, near the oars of rowers in the river, on blades of grass, are, if anything, an expansion of the wonderful achieved by miniaturizing it and setting it close by. In a similar list of examples Theodoric of Freiberg (1250–1310), who made one of the key steps toward an explanation of the rainbow, began with daily experience in saying, "It is manifest in daily experience that in spiders' webs, which are stretched out and closely covered with many drops of dew in a suitable position with respect to the sun and the eye, the colour in question, namely yellow, appears most plainly between the other colours of the rainbow in its place and order as in the rainbow; *and so close to the eye, if one wishes, that there is scarcely a hand's breadth or less between the eye and the web.*"[5] Theodoric was proving that there is a fourth color, yellow, present along with the red, green, and blue that Aristotle had mentioned as the only true colors. But in his proof he brings us, with his spider web, into a catalogue of ordinary things. The words that I have italicized highlight the need to bring the rainbow closer, along with our pleasure in doing so, and to find more occasions to study this rare and short-lived experience. Yet the spider web covered with dew, less than a hand's distance from the eye, is not less wondrous in its turn than the rainbow it replaces.

It was Theodoric who proved that the rainbow is produced inside the individual drops of rain and not by a cloud or general mist acting like a mirror that the light bounces off without entering. Each color comes from a different drop to reach the observer's eye, and inside each drop the light is refracted as it enters, is reflected off the back wall of the drop, then refracted again on exiting back to the observer, who must always be in an angle of 42 degrees between the sun and the drop of rain. The second rainbow often seen above the primary rainbow at 52 degrees is caused by rays of light having an extra reflection within the drop, thus appearing in the reverse order of colors in the second bow, which is always separated from the first by a band of unusual darkness in the sky.

This remarkable act of explanation, which was the first major addition to Aristotle in almost two thousand years, involved two distinct acts of bringing the rainbow down to earth, nearby, into the ordinary. First, as Theodoric described it, we can see that each color is produced by a separate drop by closely observing nearby events and producing small changes in them in a controlled way.

> The same thing is plainly seen also in drops of dew dispersed on the grass if one applies the eye very close to them so that the drops have a determined position with respect to the sun and the eye. Then in a particular position red appears, but when the eye is moved a little from that position yellow appears plainly and quite distinct from the other colours. Then with a further change of position the other colours of the rainbow appear in the usual number and order.[6]

On the ground near his blade of grass and single drop of dew, Theodoric positions himself in relation to the drop and to the sun behind him in the angle that begins the display of colors. Then by moving slightly so as to change the angle, he produces, in the order that they appear in the sky, the colors of the rainbow.

Theodoric's other technique is more in the tradition of laboratory science. He constructs sealed glass spheres filled with water. He has realized that these will duplicate the effects of much smaller raindrops far away in the sky. By raising and lowering a water-filled glass sphere in the path of a ray of light, Theodoric produces each color of the rainbow in turn and on command. Now he has passed from the observation of spider webs, mill wheels, and dew on blades of grass to the laboratory world of controlled experiences. The ray of light enters the sphere where it is refracted, then passes to the back wall where it is reflected back to the front wall, where it is once again refracted. Only that color reaches the eye that corresponds to the angle made by the eye, the sphere, and the light source. By raising or lowering the sphere or raising or lowering himself Theodoric produces the other colors until an angle exceeding that where a rainbow is possible has been reached and the display ends. After Theodoric the later work of Descartes or Newton will only refer to experiments done with this sealed glass sphere inside the laboratory.

With Grosseteste, Bacon, and then Theodoric of Freiberg the relation between wonder and the ordinary appears in an exemplary way. A rare and short-lived event is successfully linked to the more common and lasting everyday experiences of mill wheels, dew on grass, or water sprayed from the mouth into sunlight. A remote event that cannot be approached since it moves farther on whenever we move in its direction is seen to exist right in front of the eyes, inches away. Finally, once the principle has been grasped of the importance of the individual raindrop and what takes place inside it, a simulated raindrop is manufactured, large enough to handle, close enough to observe within a room, and enduring through time in both shape and key features so as to let the observer repeat events exactly. These are precisely the means by which the rare, unexpected, remote, and extraordinary within experience become part of the ordinary and the everyday.

At the end of this phase of explanation, the rainbow has been set inside a catalogue much broader and more experimentally precise than Aristotle's triad of echoes, rainbows, and reflections in mirrors. But in grasping the rainbow as part of the ordinary and the everyday we find anything but a dull and commonplace catalogue. In fact Keats's list of charms, angels with clipped wings, the rainbow as a woven cloth, hauntings, gnomes, and mysteries is the genuinely dull catalogue, a list of worn out poetic bric-a-brac in which a genuinely poetic experience—the rainbow—is thinly linked to an almost random set of decorative elements. Aristotle's strong pairing of echo *and* rainbow is, by contrast, a genuinely poetic act of thought, one that does exactly what we always speak of metaphor doing: captures the inner similarity of things different in appearance and remote from one another in our ordinary associations. To know that the two different experiences of hearing an echo and seeing a rainbow are similar and to express it as a moment of instantaneous perception by use of the simple word *and* is to record an intuition equal in compression, in surprise, and in deep pleasure to that of any great metaphor.

The *and* structure always defines the weak but significant intellectual structure of a list. The much stronger relation of explanation is expressed in the phrase "*X* if and only if *Y*": the statement of the causal relation. The dictionary is the most familiar instance of the entire world arranged as a list. The order of things in this list stubbornly disregards every fact but one—the order of the letters of the alphabet as they appear in the spellings of the words—in deciding which things will be side by side. Apartments are near apples, but oranges *and* apples are very far apart. Like all lists or catalogues, the dictionary breaks apart the ordinary relations of things, but in this case it creates such pointless side-by-side relations that we never consider it an important detail about a thing what it is nearby in the dictionary. Aristotle lists echoes, rainbows, and reflections in a list because he sees them as making up one genus or kind. Every genus uses the word *and* to propose a powerful reordering of the ordinary experiential world. Eventually, each new thing is inserted into one or another of the already existing clusters of things. These kinds are themselves unstable over time; things are redistributed from one to another or the kinds themselves undergo collapse or transformation. The act of insertion—into one or another of the dull catalogues of ordinary things—is the first technique of explanation. Aristotle called it determining the genus—the kind or sort—of the object. In the case of the rainbow, this act was both profound and enabling in that it made it possible to think about a spatially remote and temporally rare object by means of regular events no more than a hand's length away.

The *and* structure or paratactic structure should be seen as the most important nonnarrative relation between discrete events. The paratactic list is a modest, cautious assertion implying a common structure between the things listed. To the extent that the list is not a narrative, it can be either cautious or secretive about the actual common features that bind the objects together. If we see the paratactic list "humans, apes, rabbits, and whales," we might or might not know that a very exact theory of what characteristics define a mammal lies behind it and we might or might not know that snakes and crows would be out of place on this list. The paratactic can involve either a modest claim or a tacit but very sophisticated background theory. The alternative or hypotactic structure—which joins its elements by logical or causal terms such as if . . . then; unless; once . . . then; because; et cetera—is the narrative and therefore causal structure.

The catalogue is the first lever of explanation across which pressure is applied to the singularity of the object. It is an extensive act because, instead of looking at the object itself or its details, we set it in juxtaposition to a carefully selected set of things in the hope that common features will occur to the mind. It is important to realize that in the case of the rainbow, the key steps of explanation had nothing to do with this first step. To see the rainbow as similar to the echo will only help if the echo is already understood and its mechanisms can then be used to understand the rainbow. Aristotle's greatest mistake was his focus on the cloud as a set of small mirrors, but mirrors of a kind that reflected only color and not shape. The refraction of light, rather than its reflection—or, more exactly, refraction combined with reflection—proved to be the most important detail that led to understanding the rainbow. Refraction plays no part in either a mirror or an echo (as sound was then understood). The extensive analytic technique of cataloguing the rainbow in a category that included mirrors and echoes did not in the end yield the key details.

It was in fact the technique of substitution, an intensive rather than an extensive act, that opened the path. The catalogue overcame the rarity and the unexpectedness of the rainbow experience. It brought the essential features of that experience into a nearby and controllable space, and finally into the laboratory itself. In doing this the catalogue was itself part of the process of substitution.

Singularity and the Everyday

The experience of wonder depends at first on the uniqueness of the object. As Spinoza said, it reminds us of nothing and we are left to think only of it. One result of even the first step of explanation is to allow the uniqueness to disappear by classifying the rainbow within some set of things. But as the lists of Aristotle, Bacon, and Theodoric have shown, as we experience these lists we experience not a loss, but rather a new form of intellectual wonder. The remoteness that was at first physical, our distance from the rainbow, is now a kind of conceptual remoteness, the distance in our ordinary thoughts between spider webs and rainbows, echoes and rainbows. Our wonder that there could be any connection between the spray around an oar as it comes out of the water on a sunny day and a single drop of dew on a blade of grass as we lie on the ground nearby, and between both of those and an echo, is an experience of the genuine but unexpected interconnectedness of things. That the drop of dew three inches from my eye is connected, when I move up and down to make red, then yellow, then green, and then blue, to the necessary order of colors two miles away in the sky when a rainbow appears, is also the wonder of the link between the minute and the grand, once intermediate scales have been removed. The intimate and the celestial are set side by side.

Each of the features of wonder has been undone, but in each case in a direction that only replaces one kind of experience of wonder by another, equally sensory, but now also intellectual. The rarity and unexpectedness have been replaced once I can lie down in the grass whenever I want to look at the drop of water, but now it is the amazing link between this local, intimate experience and the sky that makes up the experience of wonder. The singularity has given way to an exact and disciplined cluster of events, but the loss of uniqueness is not noticed because of the feeling of surprise that just these things fit together and have something to do with one another. Newton's proof that a falling apple, a swinging pendulum, a cannonball's parabolic rise and fall back to earth, the moon's position and path in the night sky, and the earth's revolution around the sun were all the same phenomena replaces a wonder of uniqueness with a second wonder of a cluster of experiences so remote from one another (as they occur within our daily experience) that the act of setting them together in one thought is almost an act of violence.

In locating the extraordinary back within the ordinary, explanation breaks open the fabric of the ordinary itself and changes it forever, both for thought and for perception. The ordinary is not just the dictionary of things that we are used to; it is also the relations among them. The most primitive of these relations is what we find side-by-side in space or adjacent in time. In setting what seemed at first singular back into the ordinary we make a new ordinary only by violating contiguity, scale, and the ordinariness of genres within experience.

The rainbow's singularity can now be spelled out more exactly. That uniqueness depends on what came just before and what came just after it in time. It is a singularity of what our experience on that day led us to expect to see next. Spatially, it is a singularity over against what is to the left of it and what is to the right of it, in the same size of objects. Once our habit of thought to move along on the same scale—from horses, to dogs, to wagons, but not from horses to grains of salt, to planets—and to move within one spatial field, and to move within nearby temporal experiences; once all of these three have been set aside, there is hardly any meaning left to the idea of an "ordinary" world. These conditions of adjacency in time and place, similarity of scale, and similarity of the sector of life in which we encounter something—whether it is something to eat, or something we use in working, or something that we see usually in a church—are what we mean by the ordinary world.

The ordinary world means, in the strong sense of the word, that each thing is in its *place*. In the first experience of wonder we seem to be in the face of an object that has no *place*. But in the act of creating a place for it we do not fit it in somewhere, but find ourselves forced to undermine the nature of place altogether in order to lift many other things out of their places in order to make sense of this one. Echoes, rainbows, and our reflection in a mirror. Spider's webs, oars lifting out of water, mill wheels, rainbows, dew on blades of grass. In explanation all things lose their place so that this one new thing can seem to belong. Instead of making the singular banal or empty, setting the singular within a list of resemblances is an act that preserves the aesthetic power to strike us while at the same time dislocating the ordinary itself.

Rainbow and Raindrop: Explanation by Substitution

When Theodoric of Freiberg realized that he could make glass spheres filled with water to study indoors the paths of light in the rainbow, he substituted for the rainbow itself a more convenient object. He could only have done this because he had already understood that whatever takes place to produce the rainbow depends on how one color of the rainbow is produced in its band. He had also realized that within the band whatever happens at one point determines what happens throughout the arc of red or the arc of green as a whole. He had miniaturized or atomized the problem of the sky into the question of

what takes place inside one raindrop. Mentally he had already substituted one raindrop at the right position for the bow as a whole long
before making the second substitution of a large glass sphere filled
with water for the faraway drop that he could picture in the sky at the
site of the rainbow. Carl Boyer speculates that Aristotle could not take
this step two thousand years earlier because of his disbelief in atomis-
tic theories. As a result Aristotle thought an explanation would have
to treat the phenomenon as a whole and not its smallest imaginable
discrete part. In any case, no one before Theodoric had seen and
brought about this double substitution.

After Theodoric, explanations of the rainbow are illustrated with a
picture of the single drop and the process within it. In Theodoric's
own image only the direction of the ray of light appears as it passes
around the drop (Figure 4.1).

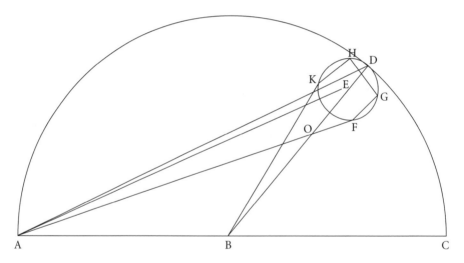

Figure 4.1   Theodoric of Freiberg, light within the raindrop.

A second illustration then positions four of these drops in a schematic landscape with the sun and the eye of the observer (Figure 4.2).
The four drops stand in for the separate bands of red, green, yellow,
and blue.

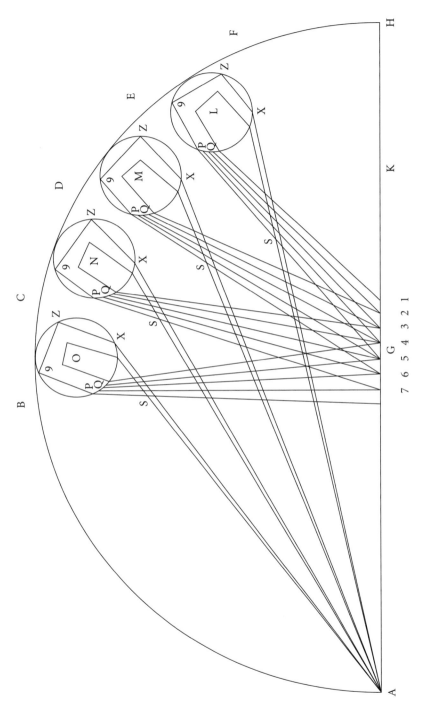

Figure 4.2 Theodoric, the rainbow, one drop for each color.

Three centuries later Descartes used the newly discovered law of refraction (whether his own discovery or borrowed from Snel is uncertain) to compute the angles within the drop and establish, among other things, why the rainbow always appears at an angle of $41\frac{1}{2}$ degrees, the angle made by the sun, the rainbow, and the eye of the observer. Newton refined Descartes's computations using the same laws to show that the primary rainbow must occur between 40 degrees 17 minutes and 42 degrees 2 minutes. The secondary rainbow always falls between 50 degrees 57 minutes and 54 degrees 7 minutes. Newton's words summing up his argument have something of the tone of God himself deciding to make the rainbow.

> *Thus shall there be made* two Bows of Colours, an interior and stronger, by one Reflexion in the Drops, and an exterior and fainter by two; for the Light becomes fainter by every Reflexion. And *their Colours shall lie* in a contrary Order to one another, the red of both Bows bordering upon the Space GF, which is between the Bows. The Breadth of the interior Bow EOF measured across the colours *shall be* 1 Degr. 45 Min. and the Breadth of the exterior GOH *shall be* 3 Degr. 10 Min. and the distance between them GOF *shall be* 8 Gr. 15 Min. the greatest Semi-diameter of the innermost, that is, the angle POF being 42 Gr. 2 Min. and the least Semi-diameter of the outermost POG, being 50 Gr. 57 Min. These are the Measures of the Bows, as they would be were the Sun but a Point; for by the Breadth of his Body, the Breadth of the Bows will be increased, and their Distance decreased by half a Degree, and so the breadth of the interior Iris will be 2 Degr. 15 Min. that of the exterior 3 Degr. 40 Min. their distance 8 Degr. 25 Min. the greatest Semi-diameter of the interior Bow 42 Degr. 17 Min. and the least of the exterior 50 Degr. 42 Min. And such are the dimensions of the Bows in the Heavens found to be very nearly, when their Colours appear strong and perfect.[7]

Newton's voice is that of the architect of the rainbow and not its humble observer. His imperative tone with its many "shall be" verbs opens up the blend of explanation and creation. Newton refines in these lines the results of Descartes, who had been the first to show why there can be no rainbow once the sun is higher than a certain point; why the angle made by the sun, rainbow, and eye must be 41 degrees and 17 minutes; why the colors are reversed in the second rainbow; and what the principle had to be behind the fact that the rainbow is a set of semicircular bands rather than an evenly illuminated half circle of light. After Descartes it was clear why the band between the two rainbows—Alexander's band—is unusually dark and why no rays were reflected above 42 degrees. And it was clear why the red band is sharply distinguished from the sky next to it while the blue has a vaguer line of separation.

What Descartes could show by means of the law of sines is that since each color will be refracted to a different point, the accumulation of enough refractions to create a visible spot of red will take place at a certain angle. Or as he puts it in his discourse on the rainbow, "And it is easy to see, in this table, that there are many more rays that make the angle of about 40 degrees than any other and that no ray makes an angle larger than 54 degrees."[8] To prove this, Descartes used a geometric diagram of the angles within the raindrop. His is the fundamental illustration in the entire history of the rainbow (Figure 4.3).

The single ray of light *EF* that strikes the drop at point *F* is refracted to point *K*, where it either exits or is reflected to *N*, where it passes out and is refracted to the observer at *P* or it is reflected once again and then passes out at *Q*, where it is bent by refraction to the observer at *R*. The many extra lines within Descartes's diagram allow him to represent how the outcome will be affected by just where the ray strikes the drop (its angle of incidence) as we imagine different rays striking everywhere along the outside circumference between *A* and *D*. In particular, the rectangle formed by *FHCD* and the unlabeled point where *DC* intersects *FG* reveals the essence of Descartes's conception of the situation. As Carl Boyer has written,

> Hence the key to Descartes' explanation is found in the idea that light is a force the vertical and horizontal components of which are independent of one another. The reflection of light from a mirror is like the rebound of a rubber ball from a wall—as Aristotle had suggested two thousand years before—and Descartes explained the equality of the angles of incidence and reflection by postulating that the velocity component horizontal to the surface remained unchanged, while the vertical component was reversed in direction. In the case of refraction he made a somewhat similar assumption—that when a ray strikes the

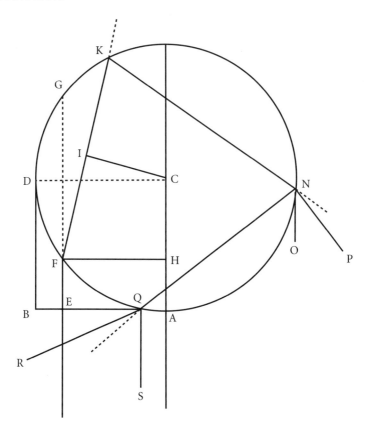

Figure 4.3 Descartes, the geometry of the ray of light within one raindrop.

surface of the denser medium, the vertical component of velocity is increased (i.e., multiplied by a constant factor k greater than unity), the horizontal component remaining the same.[9]

The rectangle allows us to consider a parallelogram of forces. And the calculation of the combination of two such refractions and one reflection let Descartes solve the question of why the rainbow is here and nowhere else in the sky and why it is only of this width.

I took my pen and made an accurate calculation of the paths of the rays which fall on the different points of a globe of water to determine at what angles, after two refractions and one or two reflections, they will come to the eye, and then I found that after one reflection and two refractions there are many more rays which can be seen at an angle of from forty-one to forty-two degrees than at any smaller angle; and that there are none which can be seen at a larger angle.[10]

Descartes's calculations and his solution depend on his earlier discovery of the law of refraction, the bending of light as it passes from one medium (air, for example) into another (water). Ultimately Descartes's drawing of refraction, a magnification and simplification of what takes place at point *F* on his main drawing, would look like the diagram in Figure 4.4. Here we might say is the grain of sand on which the entire explanation depends. In this picture the law of sines expresses the relation of the angle of incidence to the angle of refraction in terms of what Boyer has called the constancy of the horizontal (*Hi* and *Hr*) in the face of the variation of the vertical (*Vi* and *Vr*). Once this has been expressed in the equation $\sin i = k \sin r$, the calculations of the combinations of reflections and refractions can be carried out easily.

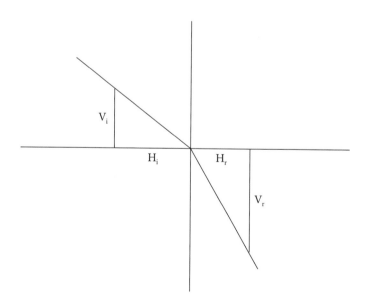

Figure 4.4 Descartes's analysis of refraction.

The sequence of substitutions is now complete. Theodoric moved from the bow to one uniformly colored band within it, then to one drop located within that band, and finally to a glass sphere filled with water. Descartes created the mathematics for this geometrical explanation by focusing on the point where the ray strikes the edge of the glass sphere. His trigonometric picture of that detail within the drop solved the central mathematical problem once he calculated for two refractions with a single reflection in between (the primary rainbow) and then for two refractions with two reflections in between (the secondary rainbow).

Newton's more elegant representation of the path within the raindrop maintains the essential lines and proportions of Descartes's drawing as well as the conclusions. His theory of color allowed him for the first time to explain the fact that a mixed light (white) strikes the drop, and yet the eye, at a certain angle, will see only green or red, yellow, or blue. The three raindrop illustrations found in Theodoric, in Descartes, and in Newton display the increasing perfection of the substitution (see Figure 4.5).

Aristotle had answered the question of whether there could be a third rainbow by denying its possibility. Newton could show where a ray that reflected three times would emerge. The third rainbow would be located across the sky from the first two, in a circular form around the sun. Because of the light of the sun, it can never be seen. But it is part of the Newtonian solution to have described invisible rainbows of three and more reflections. By the nineteenth century Josef Pernter could refine the description by showing what the consequence of different sizes of raindrops would be. In this he worked out the consequences of Thomas Young's replacement of rays of light with waves. As Boyer summarizes Pernter's work:

[Pernter] constructed tables and charts showing how the rainbow changes in appearance with changes in the size of the raindrops. For very large drops several millimeters in diameter, as in a deep tropical rain, there may be insufficient uniformity in the size to produce a rainbow (although in general uniformly large drops produce bright rainbows). If the colors of the principal rainbow arc are clear and bright, with an intense and wide violet band, and if the supernumerary arcs include rose, green, and blue, the drops causing the bow are about 1 or 2 mm. in diameter. If the red in the principal bow is weak, if there is no interval between the principal arc and the supernumeraries, and if the latter arcs include only green and violet, the diameter of the drops is about 0.5 mm. If the primary bow has no red, and if there is a narrow interval between the principal arc and the supernumeraries, the drops are about 0.3 mm. in diameter; and if yellow appears in the first super-numerary arc, the drops are not more than 0.2 mm. across. If there are several spurious arcs not well separated, and if they show only a bright violet-rose and a weak blue-green, the drop-diameter is close to 0.1 mm. . . . and if a white streak appears in the principal arc, the drops are only 0.06 mm. Finally, a white bow with a tinge of orange along the outer edge and a little blue along the inner border signifies drops of the order of 0.05 mm. . . . The white rainbow is not generally seen during a rainfall because a falling drop has a radius about ten times that appropriate for the production of a white bow.[11]

This is a point where methodical calculation and the poetry of the ordinary appear once again. By the end of the nineteenth century the rainbow's light was understood as a result of the interplay of reflection, refraction, polarization, and interference. The geometric lines that Newton used were replaced in the writings of Young and Airy by wave patterns. The expression of the whole was given by Airy's Rainbow Integral, for which diagrammatic representation is no longer useful.

The acts of substitution that we can see in passing along the history of the part played by the individual drop and the paths of a ray of light within it make clear the part played by substitution—synecdoche in rhetorical terms—within explanation. The physical substitution of one drop for the rainbow or of a glass sphere for the raindrop merges into the substitution of geometrical models, ideal and simplified shapes, angles and their relations. As Newton's description makes clear, we substitute for the sun a point source of light, and then in the end build back in a correction for the fact that the sun is a disc that is roughly half a degree in width. A single line is substituted for the bundle of rays of light, a perfect sphere for the raindrop. Finally,

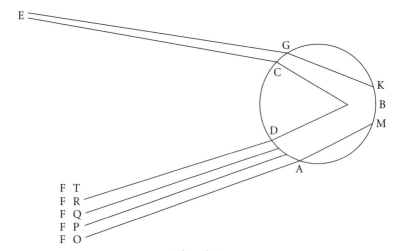

Theodoric

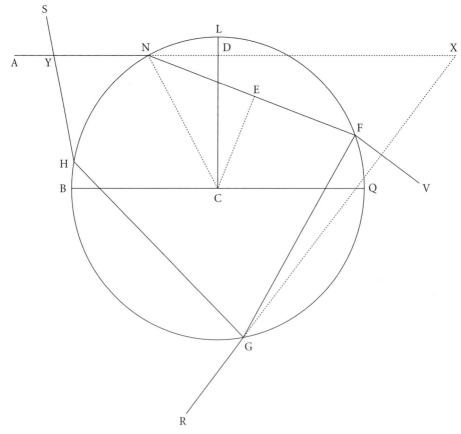

Newton

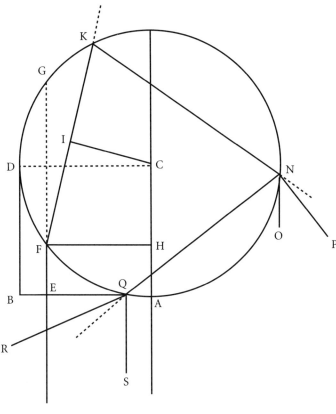

Descartes

Figure 4.5 Theodoric, Descartes, and Newton: light in a raindrop.

an artifact of thought is used—the final diagram with its many per-pendicular and parallel lines—in which only a small number of the symbolic elements (the lines and angles) any longer refer, even ideally, to actual physical details of the situation.

Inside the raindrop the major set of substitutions took place that led to the explanation that we now use for most of its features. The raindrop is the smallest necessary whole that we need to consider in grasping the band of one color—the second whole—or the rainbow itself. With Newton the set of possible rainbows—only two of them visible—composed by considering more and more reflections within the raindrop becomes, for thought, the largest unit opposite the single drop. For explanation, Newton's abstract set of rainbows was a final flourish of abstraction. The key lay in the single rainbow, the sun and its height in the sky, and the exact position of the observer.

But it has to be added that the fact of there being often a second, fainter rainbow above the first and with the order of its colors reversed was decisive in ruling out many explanations and leading to Theodoric's and finally Descartes's triumph. No theory of reflection, such as Aristotle's, could do more than explain one rainbow, with the colors in the order red, green, yellow, blue. The second rainbow, colors reversed, always 10 degrees higher in the sky, was exactly what demanded and then proved the Cartesian theory. For that reason, the explanatory history of the rainbow boils down to the miniature problem of one raindrop and the gross problem of two, reversed color rainbows 10 degrees apart in the sky. Were this second rainbow inherently invisible—as the third one is by appearing necessarily as a circle near the sun, its light lost in the greater brightness of the sun—the solution might never have been found, or rather a simpler but false theory would have been adequate.

At these two extremes—the miniature one of the raindrop and the gross one of the pair of rainbows—the intensive act of substitution was essential in the poetics of explanation. But in the larger picture, which remained more or less constant after Aristotle, we reach a refinement of substitution in which the aesthetics of experience comes into play. The raindrop itself can never be visible to the observer of a rainbow, nor is it visible in the spray around an oar in which a rainbow can be seen. The raindrops are an inference from the effect that we see—the colors. Only with the drop of dew on a blade of grass that Theodoric studied do we have present to the senses both the colors—or at least one of them and then another—and the drop at the same time.

When we stand outside on a rainy day, the sensory experience of the rainbow occurs within a crowded field of details only a few of which turn out in the end to be key ones. Aristotle's grasp of the geometry of the experience as a whole provided, for that reason, an explanation that resolved within the overdetailed moment of experience itself, the elimination of most features, or we should say, the focusing of the mind's attention to just those details that could make possible the passage from wonder to explanation.

Aristotle's grasp of the elemental facts of the overall explanation and its relative usefulness to this day occur in spite of his being wrong about nearly every detail within that larger picture. What Aristotle could see was where explanation had to take place. He created, so to speak, the blanks that would have to be filled in. That he himself filled those blanks with explanations that were wrong was less important than that he set up the very structure of the question and answer in such a way that it was immunized against the freight of mistakes that it would carry within it for more than two thousand years.

It is these two aspects of the poetics of explanation that a brief look at Aristotle's work on the rainbow can make clear: first, the passage from a crowded aesthetic experience, an experience of wonder, to a moment of tentative explanation by concentration on a few details, by substitution, and by locating the experience within a larger, but ideal—nonsensory—version of itself; second, the freezing over of unknown or false details within the explanation, its immune system, which lets it function in spite of its incompleteness—what is unknown—and its partial incorrectness—what Aristotle thinks he knows but is wrong about.

Aristotle's Geometry of the Experience of Rainbows: Explanation by Structure

Aristotle grasped the geometry of the relative positions of observer, sun, and the rainbow as a whole, and this meant that he had grasped the subjective nature of the experience, the fact that the rainbow was a visual phenomenon like the horizon line, an artifact of our human presence in the visual world. In his geometric diagram of the experience the fact of displacement or substitution will once again appear. The substitution that occurs in making a diagram alters the scale so as to collapse the gigantic onto the miniature. It disregards certain facts of distance while respecting a few others with absolute loyalty. In all diagrams of the rainbow that follow Aristotle the distance from the sun to the rainbow (93,000,000 miles) appears to be roughly similar to the distance between the observer and the rainbow (roughly 1 mile). In Aristotle's illustration he makes a necessary connection between the distance to the horizon (3 miles) and the distance to the rainbow (again 1 mile to 5 miles). In Aristotle's most important drawing the sun is imagined to be setting, resting on the horizon behind the spectator, and the rainbow is located on an imaginary celestial half-sphere that stretches over us from horizon to horizon. While fictionalizing all of these details of distance and relation, the diagram preserves for contemplation several key facts. It assembles a selection of details into one mental space at the expense of all others (see Figure 4.6).

Aristotle's explanation shows that he was struck, above all, by the regular shape of the rainbow. The half-circle that we see has to be imagined—geometrically—as generated by a radius sweeping the sky, its one end fixed at a point *P*, its other end generating, as it moves, the series of points that give us one red semicircular line within the rainbow, the arc *RZ*. Aristotle set out to define this point *P* and to explain the length of the radius *PR* that, as we imagine it sweeping the sky opposite us, would yield the rainbow at just that height where we find it in the sky.

When we speak of the line sweeping the sky there is no physical act corresponding to these words. Aristotle clearly saw the physical side of the explanation as a question of the path of a ray of light from the eye to the water drops, *OR* (the tiny mirrors so close together that they make up a continuous but irregular surface), and from there back to the sun, *RS*. The angle made by the eye, the sheet of raindrops, and the sun (*ORS*) was, he pointed out, constant. The raindrops he represented as a surface like the inside of a shiny bowl because he was considering the reflection off an imaginary celestial sphere (or bowl-like shape) that was above us from horizon to horizon. Its distance from us was the distance from the observer to the visible horizon.

The optical facts were clear to him although, like Plato, he imagined the light moving out from the eye to the object rather than the

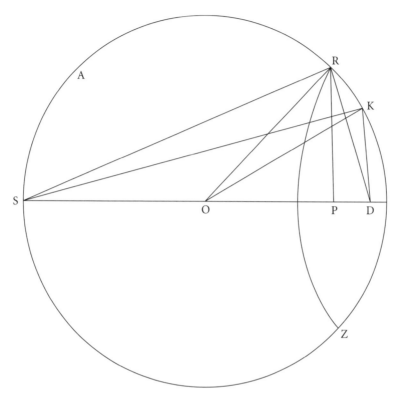

Figure 4.6 Aristotle's diagram of the sun, observer, and rainbow.

reverse. The central importance of the angle made by the sun, the continuous surface of raindrops, and the eye was equally clear and prominent. As the sun rose higher in the sky in the summer, no rainbow was possible, and when it was anywhere between the horizon and this point of impossibility, Aristotle claimed that the circle of the bow would be smaller. In fact it is not.

His geometric picture led him to consider what seem to be quite different, nonoptical actions of which the generation of the bow by the end point of a moving (imaginary) line anchored at point *P* was the most important. This point was not described by either the sun, the observer, or the rainbow itself, but it was determined by them. To find this point Aristotle considered a line drawn from horizon to

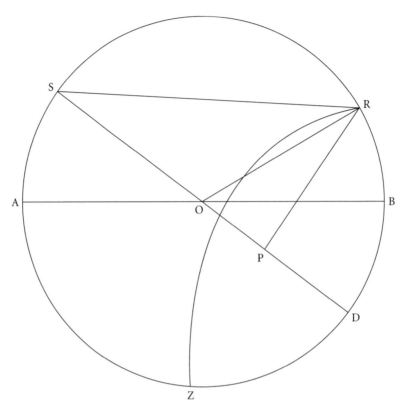

Figure 4.7 Aristotle's diagram with the sun above the horizon line.

horizon when the sun appears at the horizon. The line goes from the sun (*S*), through the point *O* of the observer, and beyond to the other horizon. If the sun were above the horizon this line would not lie on the surface of the earth but would pass from the sun (*S*) through the observer (*O*), then into the earth, where, in this case, the imaginary point *P* would be found from which the radius *PR* would, in sweeping the imagined celestial sphere, trace the rainbow, the arc *RZ* (see Figure 4.7).

The point *P* Aristotle defines by the constant ratio between the line from the sun (*S*) to the raindrops (*R*) and the line from the raindrops (*R*) to the observer (*O*): the ratio between *SR* and *RO*. Both of these lines are simultaneously geometrical and physical since they represent the path of a ray of light. The new line from R perpendicular to the line from the sun through the observer gives us this point P and the radius PR. This is not a line with optical meaning in the drawing.

In physical terms, these ratios assume that the sun is located at the horizon rather than 93,000,000 miles beyond it. They assume that once the sun has risen we can regard it as moving along a sphere that is only the horizon's distance above us. Aristotle gives a geometric explication of the location and shape of the rainbow by translating the fixed optical elements (the relative positions) into the fixed geometrical principles that govern the generation of a half-circle from a point determined by two other points (the sun and the observer). He provides no arithmetical measure, only the ratios and the geometry of the situation.

But if we consider his diagram, one of the startling facts is how similar it is to the final Newtonian diagram of the path of light inside the sphere of one raindrop. Once again, in Newton or Descartes, the fixed angular combination is expressed by a diameter line onto which the perpendiculars that we draw from the actual optical rays fall, giving a set of ratios among the segments of the diameter. Aristotle's 6-mile line from horizon to horizon—that is, the diameter of his celestial sphere where sun and rainbow are located—occurs again in Newton as the diameter line of the one 1-millimeter raindrop. The angular relations between the position of the sun, the inside back wall of the raindrop, and the observer are preserved in the complex form of two refractions with one reflection in between.

Like Theodoric of Freiberg, who understood three hundred years before Descartes what had to occur inside the single drop, Aristotle does not concern himself with the measurement. In Aristotle there is no mention of the height of 42 degrees—the position where the rainbow occurs. Theodoric mistakenly uses 21 degrees, half the correct figure, although the figure of 42 degrees was widely known in his day.

Until the refractions of different rays had been calculated as Descartes did once he had grasped the law of refraction, the actual explanation for the location could only preserve the schematic facts of the situation. This Aristotle, or whatever tradition of work he might have used for his explanation, had already accomplished. How did he do this within an explanation where most of the proof is wrong?

First, he had available to him a sophisticated geometry in which a rich store of results already existed. This geometry was his formal technology for comprehending the experience. Second, he had, in Greek optics itself, a geometrical picture in which light rays could be thought of as straight lines, and in which the light radiating out in all directions from a point source could be described as a sphere. The habit of regarding a circle or disc, like the sun or the pupil of the eye, as a point was also in place. Finally, where any one point of observation—the eye—and any light source such as the sun's disc were concerned, they defined between them a cone of light. These remarkable translations into line, point, cone, and sphere of the relations between light sources and light observers made it possible for Aristotle to picture the optics of the rainbow as the intersection of two cones of illumination, one radiating out from the point of the observer's eye, the other from the point of the sun on the horizon.

The details of the sensory experience that are preserved whatever the truth or falsity of Aristotle's explanation are the relations between sun, rainbow, and eye, understood as a fixed angle, and the locus of points that is uniquely determined by the sun and observer and by the line that runs through the sun, the observer, and an imaginary point *P*, from which a radius is produced that rotates to give the semi-circle.

From Wonder to Explanation

The final step in Descartes's small treatise on the rainbow explains how anyone who understands the principle of the rainbow can use the spray of a fountain to amaze others by producing a rainbow for their pleasure. Only those will be amazed who do not know how the effect was produced. This decline of the rainbow to the point where like a bear in a zoo it can be used for the entertainment of others and the gathering of applause to the magician who stands behind the magic show confirms the extent to which in Descartes's own thinking the path from wonder to thought to explanation is a process that brings the extraordinary into the realm of the banal and the theatrical, which among other things could be called one version of the ordinary and the everyday.

. . . .

In spite of Descartes, what I have tried to show in this analysis of the explanation of the rainbow, as in the analysis of Socrates' demonstration of doubling a square, is that there is a part secured within the process of explanation for the same triggering mechanisms that brought on attention in the first place. These wonder-preserving features of explanation can now be summed up:

First, when we undo the rarity of an experience we do so by surprising means and in unexpected directions.

Second, to bring the remote nearby is not at all to domesticate it. This is clear in the example of Theodoric of Freiberg and the drop of dew on the blade of grass.

Third, once the sudden and unexpected temporal features of an experience are outwitted by making it repeatable, the very form that repetition takes is not obvious. Its relation back to the experience being repeated is a striking one. In this case the glass sphere filled with water that we move up and down through a ray of light inside a room is the means by which we make the rainbow repeatable.

Fourth, the location of the extraordinary within the ordinary and the everyday brings about a new form of the ordinary itself that the combination echoes *and* rainbows can best represent.

Fifth, both through clustering real experiences and through substituting one experiential part for another within explanation, an aesthetic surprise is built into the result. We would be wrong not to see these acts as being among the most profound examples of metaphor, metonymy, synecdoche, and chiasmus ever produced within either thought or poetry.

Sixth, the aesthetic element of rapid change of scale from the celestial to the dustlike raindrop as we skip all intermediate scales is an element of breath-taking focus and refocus.

Seventh, the discovery within the explanation of the two key whole units requiring thought—the single raindrop and, at the other extreme, the pair of rainbows separated by 10 degrees in the sky—is a boundary problem, a question of what units within the problem have integrity and independence. It is also a result, in this case, of unexpected pleasure and intellectual complexity.

As a group these many features of the explanation are themselves a catalogue, but anything but a dull catalogue of ordinary things. They stand as elements of a poetics of disciplined thought . The part played by surprise, by the unexpected, by the moment at which attention is captured by something striking and novel, is persistent within each of these elements.

At this point as a result of the discussion of Descartes's definition of wonder and the part that he set out for wonder in shaping what we mean by having an experience, and as a result of the analysis of the part played by wonder in the steps within thought and in the larger history of the explanation of the rainbow, we can now see what is at stake in Socrates' saying "Philosophy begins in wonder." And his odd afterthought that Iris or the rainbow is the daughter of Wonder will no longer seem indulgent or merely odd as an aside.

. . . .

To this point the discussion has drawn out the aesthetic features within explanation and their close dependence on an idea of thought that cannot be separated from an idea of the passions, their energy, their state of excitement, and their temporal career of rapid or sudden appearance and slow decline.

Now I want, in the chapters that follow, to reverse the process, and, instead of beginning with learning, with steps of thought and with explanation, to begin with the aesthetics of wonder and the question of just what within certain horizons of experience is taken to be a primary and obvious instance of the experience of wonder. These aesthetic instances, which will historicize the notion of what, within any system of experience will appear as a sudden and surprising fact or event, will enable us to approach the cultural or personal force of the definition given earlier that wonder is a boundary line between the obvious, the ordinary, and the everyday, on the one hand, and the unknowable, the inexpressible, the unformulated, on the other.

FIVE

Transition to Aesthetic Wonder

Seeing What Cannot Be Seen

As we pass from a first experience of the rainbow to the curiosity that leads to the domestication of the experience, to substitutions and miniaturizations of it, and then to a model that summarizes an explanation of its effects, we remain, from beginning to end, under the instruction and under the spell of the visible. Wonder binds the mind to a visual experience that has called attention to itself by its beauty, its strangeness, and its order. Neither the strangeness nor the order can be thought of as self-evident or common to just any observer. What is strange occurs only against the backdrop of some concrete version of the ordinary, and what is meant by order refers to some highly structured notion of what counts as order. Both are cultural facts and exist as facts only for certain trained, experienced observers within the culture—not, for example, for the young children of the culture. The rainbow solicited attention and speculation within a civilization of geometry that uniquely was able to situate it at a horizon of highly ordered strangeness. Only in those cultures where Euclidean geometry not only existed but made up, at that moment, a salient of thought—Aristotle's Greece and the Europe of the seventeenth century—could just this teasing combination of the extra-ordinary and the regular have drawn thought.

The location at 42 degrees and the semicircular bands of color take effect as "regular" phenomena only in a culture of measurement and within a culture interested in the few perfect linear forms, such as the circle and the square, made by drawing an imaginary thin line around an area. Even more important, the rainbow required a culture used to imagining triangular relations among things that were not themselves triangles and among things not at all similar in nature so that the imagination supplied between unconnected things imagined as points—the sun, the eye, the rainbow—the possible triangular combinations that nowhere appear in the sky itself.

The rainbow, in other words, can make this particular claim on thought exactly because it occurs as a relation between three things (sun, rainbow, eye), not two or not seven things, because the web that might connect three things just happened to fall into the heart of the geometry of triangles, at which the Greeks were most skilled. The triangle is also the one figure where the angle is the key relation—unlike the circle, square, or rectangle—and for the rainbow the question of its angle was, in the end, the fundamental question.

What we might call the specialization of Greek civilization, its investment in a refined knowledge of what we now call Euclidean geometry, especially of the triangle and the relations among triangles, met, in the rainbow, one of its fated instances. This is a way of saying that what we call the visible is itself a horizon effect or a convergence effect. Although the rainbow was noticed and seized upon with either wonder or fear by every civilization and time, it could only pass along the chain that starts from initial attention then continues on through the curious to the intelligible among people with the habit of imagining triangles among distant and diverse objects, once they had seen, as they were primed to do, a relation among exactly three spatially remote things.

In the case of the rainbow what we mean by noticing or seeing just these three things is quite different from noticing or drawing relations among three stars seen in the night sky, or even between the moon, a ship, and a rock along the coast, objects of different types but all three located simultaneously in one observer's visual field.

The three elements sun, rainbow, and eye cannot appear in any actual visual field together. They are not seen to occupy the same space until a diagram is drawn. The sun cannot be seen by the same eye that sees the rainbow, because the sun must be at the back of the observer to produce the rainbow effect for that observer in the first place. The sun and the rainbow, by their very nature, cannot occupy the same field. No photograph of a rainbow can include a direct image of the sun that caused it.

Even more important, the third point of the triangle, the eye itself, is paradoxically never part of the same visual field as the things that it sees. The eye is invisible in a far more radical way than the sun behind the observer's back. One part of knowing that there is a triangular relation requires joining in the same visual space two things that cannot be in a visual field, but, then, to supply the third we have to—in imagination—step back from the visual altogether and no longer look at the visual field, but imagine ourselves seeing it. Aristotle's drawing, in other words, relies on our ability to step out of ourselves and picture ourselves having an experience. Since we often do this in memory, the stranger case is that we have to stand outside ourselves and observe ourselves (from just that distant point that lets the sun, rainbow, and eye occur in a simultaneous visual field) having that experience.

What we call visibility is produced by this act which goes far beyond seeing. Crudely put, there is no point of view that corresponds to the diagram of Aristotle or Descartes. The rainbow cannot be seen unless we are standing at the point represented by the observer, but from that point neither the sun nor the observer himself could be seen. The very thing represented by the diagram cannot exist as a visual state of affairs even though its essence lies in an appeal to the visible. Intelligibility lies, then, in a profound use of the visible that outwits the conditions of visibility itself. The realistic representation of a standing point and a scene in Aristotle and Descartes contains this paradoxical relation to the laws of visibility. The landscape-like scene which we see in Descartes's illustration implies the existence of a standing point from which we ourselves observe the scene with two of its three actors: rainbow, observer (Figure 5.1). The reliance of visibility on this nonexistent standing point makes evident the strong

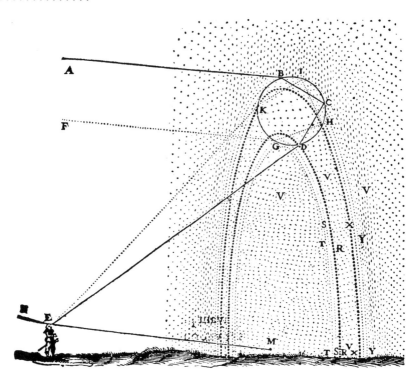

Figure 5.1 Descartes's diagram of an observer and a rainbow.

sense in which this discovered triangle that supports the visibility of the explanation is not based on any possible seen triangle.

The Visual, the Visible, and the Intelligible

In the experience of the rainbow a powerful and unmistakable appeal to the visual occurs from the first instant of surprise and pleasure at its unexpected appearance in the sky, through the process of thought and explanation, and finally in the compact geometric diagram of Descartes or Newton. This may seem an accident of the fact that Descartes and Newton preferred to give a geometric presentation of their results. Usually, we think of this preference as a seventeenth-century homage to the deductive certainty within Euclid's method. With

Newton we speak as though the geometric were a choice about how to express results, a logic of exposition and communication to others, but not a logic of discovery.

By thinking only of the step-by-step clarity of Euclid, its deductive side, we push aside what was certainly more important to Descartes and others in the seventeenth century. For them it was the part played by the visual in the instantaneous feeling of certainty that was fundamental. In the visual the complete state of affairs is present to the mind in a unique way. When we look at two side-by-side plates each of which has two apples on it, it is in one instant of time that the completely present evidence can be grasped as we say the two sets of apples are equal.

The fundamental importance of the idea of equality, whether in geometry or in arithmetic or algebraic equations, rests on this being a relation that is deeply visual and subject to instantaneous perception. Every equation is fundamentally an equal sign. As a result, in symbolic thinking no less than in the openly visual arguments of geometry where a diagram is in use, the essential final judgment is always of equality or inequality.

Naturally, ordinary circumstances are more complex than two side-by-side plates of apples. If we look at two piles of sand we cannot tell at a glance whether they are equal. We then invent a rigid, mechanical procedure. We pick up one grain at a time from each pile—one with the right hand from the first pile and one with the left hand from the other. We set the two grains aside, then pick up two more. If we finish by picking up one last grain with each hand then we can know that the two piles were equal. Each act of picking up one grain from each pile was an act of instantaneous visual certainty, and because we mechanically repeat many thousands of times the same visually certain act we feel equally certain at the end that we can say: I am confident that the two piles of sand were equal. Naturally, we can assert this even without knowing exactly how many grains of sand were in each pile, and, in fact, the exact number would always leave us uncertain of our memory or of whether we had made a mistake or lost concentration sometime during the process. Only the simple, ever repeated act can be subject to certainty. We need only know that with each step we looked to see that we had one grain in the right hand and one in the left at the same instant of time.

The conclusion that we state is not itself visual. We have only seen that one grain equals one grain again and again. Our conclusion depends on our confidence that once a complex fact has been broken down into a series of simple facts, we can mentally—but not visually—evaluate the whole by adding up our visual evaluation of each of the parts. Nonetheless, what we did, practically, was to solve an unvisualizable problem by breaking it down into many individual moments, each of which was visual and certain.

At first it might seem to be only a small further step to count out loud as we pick up the two grains of sand, saying "1" with the first act, "2" with the second, and so on. Then we would at the end of the process know not only that the two piles were equal but also that they each contained 6,329,524,307 grains of sand. But if we compare the two kinds of certainty it is clear at once that we could never be certain of this number because it would depend on remembering at each stage exactly the last number said aloud and never doubting our memory in just that kind of case where the memory fails most often—that is, when we must remember exactly a string of details in a circumstance where each detail differs only slightly from all possible wrong details. At a certain moment in the process we would have to remember that the last number said was 52,764,309 and not 52,761,309 or 52,754,309 and so on. To feel certain at the end of several months spent lifting one grain of sand in the right hand and one in the left while remembering the last number said aloud and then saying the next number exactly right is impossible. But not only is it possible to be certain that the two piles were equal and that each time—even over months of work—I had lifted one and only one grain with each hand, glanced at them as I set them aside, and felt certain of their equality I was correct, but that possibility and certainty underlie every circumstance of certainty whatsoever. To arrive at the final number in addition to the certainty that the two piles were equal requires at every step two quite different kinds of certainty, the one visual, the other a certainty of the memory in calling up the last number exactly and then saying the next one exactly even when the numbers become ever longer. This simultaneous tax on the memory and on the visual intuition creates a complex situation in which no certainty is possible.

We could repeat at a more complex level the relation of the visual to certainty by examining in slow motion the visual details of Newton's diagram of the raindrop. Why does the visual play this part in securing certainty while at the same time capturing, in an experience of pleasure and absorption, a model for relation to the world per se? The slogan of Stevinus—Wonder drives out wonder—actually appeared in his own work above a diagram of his major discovery. The diagram itself is a nearly perfect instance of the relation of the visual to a kind of clarity and instantaneity that came to define certainty itself. Stevinus' discovery was of the relation of forces on an inclined plane. His thought experiment, or diagram, uses a triangle on which a freely moving chain of spheres stands at rest or moves until it is in equilibrium. Since the spheres are of equal weight the relation of forces is evident at once when we compare the number along the left side—call it *ab*—to the number on the right side—call it *bc* (see Figure 5.2).

Figure 5.2 Stevinus' diagram of forces on an inclined plane.

This brilliant image of the relation of the forces to the lengths to the angle of the plane sums up all of Archimedes' work on a ball rolling down an inclined plane and divides the force of gravity into two components in an instantly comprehensible way. The number of spheres on side *ab*—four in the diagram—must be in equilibrium with the number on side *bc*—two in the diagram. The force of gravity is inversely proportional to the length of the plane. The parallelogram of forces, the vertical and horizontal components of each force, have been divided visually. The diagram condenses and expresses with clarity and certainty the entire mechanical system.

If either plane *bc* or plane *ab* were perpendicular to the base, the relation of the number of spheres on the remaining plane to the force of gravity (the free fall represented by the perpendicular plane) would be clear as well. Stevinus' diagram is not the illustration of an experiment; it is instead an ideal case, a thought experiment. Although his motto suggests that understanding the relation of the rolling ball to gravity will bring wonder to an end, his own diagram suggests that it redirects wonder from the facts of nature to the act of discovery. Now we are amazed by the human powers that in an instant of time saw the logic of the complex situation in this simple and elegant way after almost two thousand years in which again and again minds had returned to contemplate the work of Archimedes. The diagram becomes the monument to this moment of insight and our wonder, almost four hundred years later, is still aroused by it. So proud was Stevinus of this image of what he called the *clootcrans* that he used it as a seal on his letters, as a monogram on all of his instruments, and as the figure on the title page of his books, where above it appear the words, "Wonder en is gheen wonder."

The intellectual analysis of the visual reaches a provocative climax in Descartes, where the entire meaning of certainty and of clear and distinct ideas follows from his replacement of deductive certainty, which must ultimately take place over time and with the aid of the memory, with the certainty that Descartes calls intuition. Within experiences of intuition, Descartes recognizes two possibilities, visual intuition and intellectual intuition, but, as he points out, the very term that he is using means, in Latin, seeing. Intuition does not, in

Descartes, refer to our modern sense of a hunch or a feeling that one knows something without being able to prove it. Instead, it is an instantaneous moment of seeing, like that of discovery or of wonder itself.

In his first book, *Rules for the Conduct of the Understanding,* Descartes makes a number of striking proposals for a universal method of thought. In this small book he speaks of the human mind or spirit as composed of four faculties: sense, memory, imagination, and understanding. The basic act of the understanding is the instantaneous act of intuition, of certainty. Descartes defines intuition in this way: "By intuition, I mean, not at all the unstable report of the senses, nor the deceptive judgment of the imagination which operates with compositions that have no value, but a representation that is made by the pure and attentive intelligence, a representation so simple and so distinct that there can remain no doubt about what we understand in it; or, what comes to the same thing, a representation inaccessible to doubt, a representation that is the result of the intelligence in a pure and attentive state, a representation born uniquely from the light of reason, and that, because of its greater simplicity is even more certain than deduction."[1]

The pure and attentive intelligence faced with something that is itself simple characterizes our basic experience of the presence of something. In this it is like the experience of wonder. As examples of intuition Descartes lists the fact that "each of us can see by intuition that he exists, that he thinks, that a triangle is delimited by only three lines, the sphere by only one surface, and other similar things that are much more numerous than most people think because they disdain to turn their minds to things so simple."[2]

The single example that Descartes examines at length is a shrewd one. We must see, he claims, by a certain intuition that 2 plus 2 equals 3 plus 1. In this we must intuitively see four distinct things with equal clarity. First, that 2 plus 2 equals 4, and for this we might use a visual diagram to let us see the truth at a glance. Second, we must see that 3 plus 1 equals 4, and here too a visual diagram will work. The third certainty is a result of the first two. It is the intuition that $2 + 2 = 3 + 1$, but this can best be represented visually by retaining a picture of 4 in the middle between the two sets, even though in the equation itself the number 4 does not appear.

For the actual fact before us there can be no real diagram because it is not an independent fact but one that we feel certain about because it follows the first two equations. We need also a fourth certainty: that our third equation follows necessarily from the first two. If they are true, it must be as well. Here we reach the nonvisual intuition that is similar to the final step with the piles of sand. We have seen only that each time one grain of sand equals one grain of sand. The final step in which we say that since each of the grains had a partner, the two piles must be equal, involves us in a new order of certainty that has no visual element.

The visual element within intuition in these examples depends on the central relation of equality, a fundamentally visual experience. At the same time, we might notice that one of Descartes's hidden motives is to eliminate both imagination and memory from the act of thought. The instantaneous quality of intuition is one of its essential features. It is a here-and-now experience of presence—the one grain of sand in my right hand, the one grain of sand in my left, and with both hands seen at the same instant by my eyes.

Ruling Out Memory

Both memory and imagination are forms of presence for what is not actually present to the senses here and now. Memory is one of the great antagonists for Cartesian intuition and for the aesthetics of wonder. In a preliminary way we can see just how destructive memory can be for thought when we realize that at every step if we are reminded of something we are in effect distracted from pure and complete intellectual attention. The essence of religious argumentation lay in always being reminded of some relevant biblical quotation. The part played by authorities in argument—that is, by references to the words or arguments of someone whose very name is intended to carry conviction without any analysis of the exact argument itself—is a sign of the importance of memory within argument for cultures of quotation and reference to authority. Memory is essential if you believe that we already know everything knowable because in that case every uncertainty must be solvable by remembering it ourselves or by asking an authority who does remember it.

If everything has already been explained (by authorities), we only have to remember what it was that they said the explanation was. Memorization is a system of education exactly opposite to the scientific education for discovery that is Descartes's goal. In systems of memorization, we have to remember the proverb or law of which this apparently new instance in the here and now is in fact just one more example. Memory is the fundamental faculty for an already fully known world of experience. It depends on each new thing reminding us of something that we already know. Here again, the essence of the moment of pure presence within wonder lies in the object's difference and uniqueness being so striking to the mind that it does not remind us of anything and we find ourselves delayed in its presence for a time in which the mind does not move on by association to something else.

A second feature of memory for Descartes is its unreliability. As Descartes says in his key Rule 16, if all thinking is a combination of visual intuition and intellectual intuition, then thinking can still seem to need memory to keep all the relevant facts in front of it, but to do this we would have to "immobilize part of our attention to keep the memory accurate, at the cost of other thoughts," and therefore

> art has very happily added the use of writing, thanks to the use of this latter, we confide absolutely nothing to memory, and we preserve completely all of our free play of thought for the ideas that are present in front of us by inscribing on a paper all of that which we have to retain, and we do that by means of signs that are so concise so that they can be passed distinctly in review one after another (in conformity with Rule 9) and run through them by a very rapid movement (as in our Rule 11) thus taking in the largest possible number among them in a simultaneous intuition.[3]

To make a diagram or even a set of notes in a list form, we use the memory but then displace it by now putting in front of our eyes all the relevant facts. Writing transfers the successive into the simultaneous, and as we move from a list to a diagram or to an algebraic symbolism we push ourselves toward a more and more simultaneous presence of what had to be in the memory a successive series of facts, some distant by many seconds or minutes from one another in any review of the whole set. In the memory only two things can be directly adjacent to each other, but on a sheet of paper many elements can have this relation of being side by side or next to each other. Certainty is possible when simultaneous presence of the question and the answer can occur to the eyes and to the mind. In his summary at the end of his key Rule 16, Descartes is even more emphatic: "One must never confine anything to the memory of that which does not demand a constant attention if one can put it on paper; it must not happen, in effect, that a superfluous effort of the memory robs one part of our mind from the task of knowing the object present to it."[4]

The simultaneous intuition is once again possible only in a visual space. Symbolism crowds together the elements of thought until the eye has them all available at once. The only clarity, distinctness, simplicity, and certainty are those of the eye. Visual experiences like that of the grains of sand or that of $2 + 2 = 4$ can be gone over again and again until they provide the template for a feeling of certainty that can then be tested in Descartes's more complex instances of certain intuition—for example, that I exist, that I think.

It is important that the examples that we have in mind are not only taken from mathematics, although by this point it should be clear that it is not some fugitive mathematical certainty per se that Descartes and Newton are appealing to, but rather the built-in acknowledgment of the visual and the instantaneous that mathematical thinking incorporates.

A remarkable, nonmathematical example of visual certainty is the perception of symmetry. When we look at an object and intuit that it is symmetrical we make a very complex judgment about it, but one that depends only on what is present fully to the eye at one glance. There is no meaning, for example, in calling a building symmetrical or a town symmetrical if there is no standing point and angle from which it can be taken in at a single glance. Sometimes we produce a map of a town that reveals its symmetry, but in experience itself, until the invention of the airplane, this was not a fact about it, just as

symmetry is not a "fact" about the floor plan of a symmetrically arranged apartment, although any architect's drawing would show it to
be a symmetrical arrangement of rooms around a central hall. In fact,
to be in the apartment we have to be in one or another room. Our
eyes can only see the one room that we are in. We might remember
that across the hall we had earlier been standing in a room like this
one, with windows in a similar location along the wall, but we would
have to go back to that room to check details and then we would be
comparing those details with our memory of the room that we had
just left. The apartment as a whole is not "symmetrical" because there
is no visual experience possible that would give us the instantaneous
intuition of this visual fact.

Pascal called symmetry "what we see at a glance[,] [b]ased on the
fact that there is no reason to do otherwise. And based too on the
human face, which is why we want symmetry only in breadth, not in
height or depth."[5] Only horizontal symmetry as in buildings or human bodies can ultimately count under this instant certainty because
the template experience from which all instantaneous intuitions of
symmetry derive is our attention to the human face and figure, and
even in that case, only when we see it face to face at a certain angle
and distance. If we are too close there is no symmetry (as in passing
over the surface of someone's face with a magnifying glass), and when
we are too distant, say half a mile away, there are no visible pairs of
features and therefore no symmetry.

The experience of symmetry is only one of a wide range of instantaneous effects of visual intuition that are on the one side intellectual
and on the other aesthetic. Let me give only one other important
experience: consider the visual pleasure of a radical disproportion of
scale—a very large man with a tiny dog on a leash or an enormous
wall with only a tiny window in it. This effect is often comic, and
laughter is one of the most basic clues to a sudden experience of
"getting it" or to an instantaneous visual experience of distinct things.
Descartes, in describing the physical effects of the passions in his final
book, spoke of the first cause of laughter as the surprise of wonder
(*l'admiration*) in cases where joy was present. But the visual experience of a radical disproportion of scale also works to move us in ways

that have nothing of wit or slapstick about them. In a painting where, within many somber colors and an overall shadowy effect, there is one rare and precious area of brilliant red we experience the same instantaneous visual intuition. It is only the extremity of the disproportion of colors, a disproportion that is uniquely present to the mind because all of the colors are seen at one glance, that makes the intuition of rarity and drama possible as we look at the painting.

These effects of symmetry and radical disproportion make clear the most complex and lively activity of sensory and intellectual energies within instantaneous experiences where presence is the primary category. Within the faculties of absence—memory and imagination—no such effects of simultaneity have force. In memory and imagination there must always be juxtaposition, simply because these two faculties operate in time and because they are free of the controls that presence imposes on juxtaposition. Free play and recombination are more common in the memory and in the imagination just because they are less costly. We can imagine a blue face or remember an elephant and then a mouse, but these combinations are not telling or exciting in the way that their existence in the visual field as a simultaneous and present experience would be. The imagination is all surprises and therefore lacks any genuine meaning of "ordinary" against which the extraordinary could be experienced.

Wonder, knowing, and intuition, once we understand them in this very specific Cartesian way, share with aesthetic experience this exploitation of simultaneity, that is, of a form of unity that cannot be expressed among diverse things except by the fact that there is, literally, a visual experience in which this unity occurs. The experiences of equality, symmetry, and radical disproportion of scale stand here for a wide variety of aesthetic features that are closely related to wonder and to certainty, and are limited to those experiences in which the intellectual or aesthetic whole exists at one glance. This suggests that the use of diagrams in mathematics and the arrangement of visual symbolism within proof underlines a uniquely intellectual aesthetics of painting and architecture because they are the only two art forms that make use of the instantaneous effect of the whole.

SIX

Intelligibility, Wonder, and Recognition

Rainbow, Explanation, Error

If we examined in turn each of the diagrams that summarize the explanations of the rainbow from Aristotle to Descartes, we would be struck by the limited damage done by incomplete or false information. In one diagram of Theodoric's all four colors seem to be produced by rays of light moving within a single raindrop. Before Newton, no one operated with a correct theory of color—that white light was composite. Before Young no description assumed a wave theory of light. Theodoric used 21 degrees for the elevation of the rainbow in the sky, half the correct value of 42 degrees, even though the latter figure was widely known in his time. Aristotle describes reflections rather than the double refraction flanking a reflection that is the explanation after Theodoric.

These mixtures of knowledge, ignorance, and error about what we know, what we think we know but are wrong about, what we know that we don't know, and what we haven't even thought about yet because it hasn't been raised—what we don't even know that we don't know—are found everywhere in the process of explanation.

In Socrates' discussion with the boy about doubling the square, the silence about the length of the side after a certain point in the discussion is one possible relation to the partial and damaged process of explanation, which is, we might say, undefeated by error or ignorance.

The explanation is partially successful, as are all the explanations and accounts of the rainbow. There is not any simple passage from wonder to explanation, question to answer. Instead there is an unfurling of knowing and curiosity that finds itself at every moment in mixed conditions. Only the biblical or mythological style of narrative meaning locks into place an answer to which we can respond: so that's what it *really* is.

The messy explanatory situation that we found both in the *Meno* problem and in the explanation of the rainbow, the result of what I have called the half-way horizon between the everyday and the unknowable where wonder occurs because thinking or curiosity is enabled, but not easily satisfied or quieted—this half-way stage is the stage of the knowable, not of the known. The magnet, that other conspicuous instance of wonder throughout the same period as the rainbow, rested outside that half-way stage until the nineteenth century, when theories of electricity and magnetism brought it at last into the middle distance that, because of geometry and the knowledge of light and color, the rainbow had occupied since at least Aristotle's time. The messy explanatory situation is, nonetheless, the location of fruitful wonder and curiosity, a location which many other phenomena—such as the magnet until the time of Faraday and Maxwell—remain outside.

What I am calling the limited damage of error, equivocation, silence, evasion, and simple blank places in explanation within the model proposed by Cartesian wonder points to the place where this poetics of thought opens out into our more risky and inconclusive knowledge or confidence about works of art. With the art of our own time we find ourselves, as Galileo described himself in the *Starry Messenger* of 1609, seeing and making sense of things never seen or known before by any man or woman in history. With these works we face so constantly the conditions of novelty, surprise, strangeness, and power that rather than wonder we might suspect we are feeling some fatigue of wonder, some overdraft on the account of wonder in our spirits, some routinization of the very psychic power that stands as the last alternative to the routine and to the familiar. In a secularized world we might also be saying, "When the salt has lost its savor, with what can it be salted?"

Even within the parade of the odd and the fantastic in our art the claim made at the beginning of this book seems to me to remain true. The visual art of the twentieth century—architecture, sculpture, painting, assembly, installation—has worked from an aesthetic of wonder rather than an aesthetic of memory and recognition, and it has triumphed with its strangeness, novelty, and attention-seizing un-expectedness. It has often done so by means of what I think of as thirty-second art, works of a single, overall point which we can absorb in half a minute even if critics, talk about them for hours, days, and years. Marcel Duchamp's urinal, many works of slogan and reading-art are of this kind. Attention is seized, used up, and dismissed in a brief single-minded cycle.

But where the intricacies of wonder play themselves out in long detailed engagement with the work, I want now to show that the aesthetics of wonder imposes an intricate process remarkably similar to the steps of problem solving that we have already examined in the case of the doubled square and the rainbow. Can it really be said that we are, in Descartes's sense, in a state of wonder with a work of art? Does the surprise and novelty arouse curiosity and a desire to know? Is there, then, a point at which we know the work? I hope that I have prepared for this question by reducing or making more equivocal the sense in which we know the rainbow or know how to double the square. We do not have, nor do we seek to have, a right answer that abolishes the question, makes it uninteresting. Unfortunately, it might seem that it is just with works like the Duchamp urinal that we do pass through the baffled surprise, exploration, and then certainty of "getting it," knowing in a rather simple way what it means to find this work in a museum gallery. There is clearly an answer that puts curios-ity to rest, and rather quickly—under a minute or two, I would guess. Someone else can even tell us and we can say, "Now I get it!" and that's all there is.

The dilatory process of wonder has other instances, among them our first encounter with an unexpected work of art, and the poetics of this process is also a poetics of thought. Its outcome is a kind of intelligibility or partial intelligibility that has been subsidized and led on by wonder.

To explore this second path, I want to turn to the experience of wonder and its path to intelligibility and thought within aesthetic experience. Up to this point I have tried to show that within thought there is a deep component of the aesthetic. The heart of that blending of thought and pleasure is identified by the experience of wonder. In the argument that follows I want to move in the opposite direction. In works of art, where we certainly agree in advance that there is pleasure and aesthetic excitation, can we also show that the essence of this aesthetic component is a process of thought and active thinking closely related to discovery in science? Where we earlier started from thinking and found wonder and the poetics of thought, can we now start from aesthetic pleasure and find the exactness and sequential pleasures of thought and its drive toward intelligibility, its passage from curiosity to the satisfaction of intelligibility?

To get to the question of wonder and its part in the process and reach for intelligibility in our experience of a work of art, I need first to consider and put aside the alternative to wonder, memory and recognition. We commonly think that recognizing something, or connecting it to some other realm that we already know, is the primary source of intelligibility and the feeling of comfort in our relation to art. If we recognize the work we feel that we "get it." Nothing could be more damaging to a real account of the aesthetics of our experience of a work of art than this equation between recognition and intelligibility. Before beginning my own argument that wonder and a type of problem-solving thinking lie at the heart of the best account of intelligibility of a work of art, I will first look at the alternative, the claims of memory and recognition.

Recognition: Can Only Memory Guide Intelligibility?

As John Keats in his "Ode on a Grecian Urn" gave his excited inspection of the urn, he faced a work of art with just that puzzled and half-defeated mood that spells the onset of a troubled relation between audience and art in modern culture. Put quite simply, Keats can't be certain just what it is that he sees, and he can't be certain what it is that he is to do with it. Keats can only fleetingly recognize what is in front of him. For each of the scenes that he describes he knows this but not that, and he never knows the whole intended artistic fact. "What men or gods are these?" He can recognize that he is in a world that has men and gods—polytheism—but he cannot tell whether these are men or gods—he has lost iconic confidence, and even if he could say that much he still does not know their names, their stories, or their purposes here on this urn. "What men or gods are these?" Such a question—and it is only one of dozens in the poem—comes out of a pathos of intelligibility in culture, one that slowly undoes the difference between "our culture" and all else, between an actual tradition humming underneath the present and a set of mere facts with which we might or might not happen to be acquainted.

Many acts in the face of a work of art can be termed recognitions. John Keats recognizes that the object in front of him is an urn and he recognizes that it is from ancient Greece. Looking at a painting we recognize that this is a woman and we recognize that that is a religious painting. We recognize another painting as a still-life, a genre recognition. This work we recognize as seventeenth-century Venetian, that as a 1960s "happening." Another we recognize must be by Matisse, one of his Morocco paintings. Yet another we recognize as a Cubist painting, and in the painting we recognize a certain detail as guitar, or as an actual fragment of a newspaper. Picasso recognized the image of a bull in a bicycle seat and handlebars joined a certain way, and we do the opposite step when, on seeing his bull, we recognize that it really is a bicycle seat and handlebars as we get closer in the gallery. Our surprise replicates by inversion his first moment of seeing.

Recognition defines the part played by memory in visual experience, and in the discipline of art history it sums up the part of iconography and iconology, Erwin Panofsky's key terms. Long postponed recognition is one of Aristotle's two most important aesthetic effects—recognition and reversal—within a tragic plot.

Recognition is the means by which we differentiate "our tradition" from mere works, or from what we know to be someone else's culture.

With our own tradition we recognize most or all of the details, with African carved objects, few or none. The design of works around recognitions, the salting of the mine of the work with dense clusters of recognizable clues, mentions, and suggestions, all of which work for those inside and come up blank for those outside the culture, is one of the essential features of a certain idea of having a culture at all.

I would like to make an oversimplified distinction between three groups of works. First are the works of all other cultures about which we can become learned and effective, but which we cannot, in some simple everyday way, recognize, meaning by this word that we cannot generate a wealth of individual recognitions and come to feel, by that means, that the work is intelligible to us. The second group is made of the works that we call our own past, the culture for which in time and space, the act of recognition is rich, detailed, and easy. The third group is made up of radically new works produced in our own time with which we are unfamiliar, which we cannot place in genres or patterns of knowledge. In these new works we could say that, whatever seeing amounts to, it does not primarily involve recognition. The work comes up blank.

Let me say first of all: these new works share with the works of other cultures the fact that recognition is a less and less significant part of what we do as we look at them. Roland Barthes singled out works that he called "le nouveau absolu"—"the absolutely new"—as the center, in any experience of art, of aesthetic pleasure. He pointed out that as readers we enjoy and spend most of our time away from such works. What we easily enjoy is the language just before the present, the "next-to-the-last language." As a reader he found himself sunk into evenings with Zola, Proust, Verne, or the imitators and extenders of their language and narrative procedures into the present. This language, which he called "the language I speak *within myself*," is already mapped language, already inhabited language—habit-ridden language—the language not of our times. To escape from this inhabited language Barthes drives himself to write. "I write," Barthes put it, "because I do not want the words that I find [those that I already have]."[1] What we find already going on is a language of formulations for which we are supposed to be happy to discover more and more instances, variations, or negations. Formulation is one variety of recognition: he is a gentleman; he is not a gentleman; he is a gentleman but rough and of the people—"of the people" being yet another formulation, just as "gentleman" was.

After modernism we are likely to make a mistake about the phrase "the absolutely new," taking it to refer to odd, obscure, or opaque and totally baffling works like *Finnegans Wake* or the poetry of Gertrude Stein. We need to return to the point where we can remember that Stendhal's *Red and the Black,* Dickens's *Pickwick Papers,* Scott's *Waverley,* Austen's *Pride and Prejudice,* Richardson's *Pamela,* Goethe's *Sorrows of Young Werther,* were absolutely new. In Barthes's sense it is not only the odd or the marginal, *Tristram Shandy* and e. e. cummings, that are at the moment of their appearance and against the horizon of experience, absolutely new. And just as the world is new for every fifteen-year-old Miranda, these works, *The Red and the Black,* the essays of Montaigne, the paintings of Cézanne are "absolutely new" for each of us at some point in our experience. Barthes is not leading us to value odd or obscure works, but rather to push aesthetic priority away from knowledge, meaning, genre, and formulation toward the first moment we saw one of Michelangelo's unfinished slaves, the first hearing of the second act of Mozart's *Marriage of Figaro.* He is not promoting that tricky kind of avant-gardist work whose intention is to have so simple and unexpected an effect that it can mainly exist to be mentioned, to be brought up again and again in discourse, a work of art that is a scandal or merely a topic.

What Barthes's category of the "next-to-the-last language" isolates is the sphere of recognitions, whether affirmed, nuanced, equivocated, or denied. "Ceci n'est pas une pipe." This is not a pipe. When you are tired of recognizing, try denying and see if that will keep the stale game fresh a minute or two longer.

What Keats finds with his Grecian urn is that it is only the "just past" that we can recognize fully. The past of the past, the long ago, the just-before-the-just-past is already quickly fading. With his barrage of questions, conjectures, recognitions, and puzzles Keats dramatizes for us the fact that the intelligibility of works of art recedes over time and that we can speak almost mathematically about the number of recognitions and of their diminution, century by century. When we look at the great works of Poussin in the Louvre we find ourselves very much like Keats, knowing that someone once could recognize this or that detail, but we are left to say, "What men or gods are these?"

Paradoxically, over time, as recognitions decline, the works of what we call "our own" culture fall into exactly the same relation to us as the one we have to works of all other cultures—African masks, a Japanese screen, a set of sculptures on Easter Island—objects where recognition fails, objects about which we have no anecdote, no allegory, no clue to social purpose, subject, or proper aesthetic comportment. All of these works require an idea of intelligibility different from one based on recognitions.

Although the three categories of works of art converge, our choice of which of the three to make salient for an investigation of aesthetic experience involves very important differences. Descartes had the very important idea that we need to practice the feel of certainty. We need to go over and over again through simple cases like the statement "Two plus two equals three plus one" or "A triangle has three sides" so that we can fund or secure our new experiences of certainty on the basis of knowing what certainty feels like. Similarly, with art we need to be clear about what kinds of experience let us fund our idea of intelligibility, confidence, relaxed ease with a work.

Barthes made the radical claim that it is with the art of our own time that we need to begin, practice attention, weigh "the absolutely new." He was proposing a discipline of wonder and a training that required every critic to spend a large fraction of her or his time with as yet undescribed works, unplaced works. In this, I believe that Barthes was right. Our common assumption that the salient experience for aesthetics should be the typical experience with a rich work from the past of our own culture, from what we call the "tradition" or the "canon," is wrong.

Iconology, iconography, ideology, the study of allegory and anecdote, history and meaning insist on the central place of the "next-to-the-last" in culture, Barthes's next-to-the-last language. It is sometimes forgotten that if we care to historicize, even to New-Historicize, we can only effectively do so within a certain zone of the past. The entire past is not history. Some is too close. Agreed-upon categories have not yet fallen into place. Most of the rest of the past is too far away. The nineteenth century and the Renaissance are the outer borders for most of what we call history, ideology, iconography, and iconology. These are the sciences of the language just before the present.

The choice in literary culture over the past twenty-five years has been to make salient precisely this next-to-the-last language. We might ask why the analytic attack of New Historicism and deconstruction favored—even required—works of art that had been too much discussed, too often read, works with layers and layers of familiarity and familiar conclusions. Each of these methods thrived on being late in time, arriving when a kind of fatigue had taken over, so that now one could be paradoxical, could read all the earlier readings and strike sparks off the layers of accumulated readings of readings.

New Historicism looked again, and often from a strikingly fresh analytic angle, at some of the most overanalyzed works of art that we have: the English Renaissance, Romantic poetry, the few writers of the American Renaissance, Spenser. This knowing lateness felt like mannerism, like the ingenuity and paradox of paths too often traveled, a critical decadence.

Neither deconstruction nor New Historicism had any leverage on new work, the work of our time, work not yet read, classified, identified. Both were archeological relations to culture; they needed instances that were comfortably past. One characteristic of this whole generation of critics in literature is that they have been silent about the work of their own time. In the previous fifty years the works of the present drove the angle of attention to the past, and there was a rich and sophisticated, but highly risky, engagement with each stage of the work of writers in the present.

Critical styles like deconstruction and New Historicism—the styles of revisionists—had nothing to say about the present. They saved critics from the problem of how to think out loud in not yet articulated realms of experience, what we might call pre-mature aesthetics and criticism rather than belated, late in time, revisionary criticism.

The new and the unformulated are exactly those realms where the aesthetics of wonder and other strong experiences of the unexpected, the unplaceable, the radically new are necessary guides to attention, curiosity, and the process of creating intelligibility.

The Newness Effect in Modern Art

The act of recognition, multiplied into a wealth of individual recognitions and recognitions of variations, makes up our normal path to intelligibility with a work of art. But within the art of our own century we often find ourselves coming up short when we look into the work to recognize figures, anecdotal materials, genres that seem familiar ones: portrait, landscape, still-life, altarpiece. Keats sees that we no longer know, but at least he does know what it is that he ought to know. We find ourselves baffled not knowing what it is we are supposed to know or to do. The intertextual link back to earlier art of two or three centuries ago often seems weak or absent. How is this object in a Soho gallery like a Titian, or some project Raphael would have undertaken? What does this have to do with Dürer, Rembrandt, Poussin, or Vermeer?

We might go further and ask a stronger question. Why it is that the works of artists in our time look so different not just from the art of the past, but from each other. Why are these works so distinct? They differ more from one another than one person does from another. Why should that be possible, since any two works were made by human beings, by Americans of a certain decade and often of a certain class? Why should these works look as though they were the products not of different men and women, or even of different cultures, but of different species, as we might imagine works of art would differ were they made by sparrows and apes, grasshoppers and whales, or even art made by trees would differ from art made by wind? If people were as radically different from one another as species are, then we would expect every work of art that embodied the sensibility and experiences of its artist to be as different from any other as the artifacts dreamed up by a hummingbird would be from those invented by a turtle.

In other arts we do not find this. Men and women have written novels over many centuries and within many cultures, many classes and historical circumstances. The outcome has been a remarkably stable and self-similar genre, which does in fact allow for and express many ranges of experience and style. Novels differ from one another just about as much, but no more, than people do. The paintings of Raphael, Michelangelo, Titian, Masaccio, Giotto, Piero della Francesca, and Botticelli differ among themselves within about the same range as novels do, and I would say about as much, but no more, than men and women do in outlook, sensibility, purposes, intelligibility. In social life behavior is scrutable because it falls within a limited range. These banal facts say nothing more than that we might expect human art to have only a certain range of difference. There is a fundamental implausibility about the idea that works of art would not fall into genres and similar types just because people are more the same than different. Their core experiences are more alike than unlike. The difference between the art of Cézanne and that of Poussin is more plausible than the difference between Richard Serra and Henry Moore, Dan Flavin and Claes Oldenburg.

The question has another side. Once we have seen one of Richard Serra's massive steel-plate sculptures and wish to see others, ten, twenty, fifty, we find that each is only slightly different from the last. Why are they so much alike? Why are Giacometti's hundreds of figures so similar, especially given that they began by seeming so wondrously different from anything seen before? How do we pass so quickly form wonder to boredom when we see a major retrospective, a one-man or one-woman show by Louise Nevelson, Henry Moore, Richard Serra, or Joan Miró?

Why is the internal differentiation so shallow? Has all of the energy been expended in reaching a starting point where the work is so radically unlike the work of others that, once this has been accomplished, the rest is mechanically spun out in near-duplication? One of the most obvious features of the art of our time is not what Walter Benjamin called mechanical reproduction. Instead we live in a time of quasi-replication, near duplication of works too much like one another, as though to satisfy the market need to have "one of these" here in San Francisco, one there in Houston, and so on. The artist makes what we might call a batch: using the same recipe, but making each work distinct enough so that each collector can have his own slightly different but still recognizable example.

The paradox of batch production of slightly different similar works is the other side of the first problem, the excessively individualized starting point for any one artist's identity. That first problem seems driven by the requirements of wonder, surprise, the feel of unprecedented works, newness, and delight in works that puzzle, that invite curiosity and the search for a new path for intelligibility.

We seem deprived of those many local recognitions that would have set in motion familiarity, a feeling of variation, a certainty about the artist's goals and our behavior in the face of those goals. To look thoughtfully at a work by Poussin meant to travel through it led on by recognition and by difference—crudely put, by the large-scale logic of variation for which the tradition provided the dictionary behind this new work.

If we do not travel through the work in this way, how do we manage to spend time with a modern work, an abstract work without iconographic or iconologic clues? If we compare a painting to a rainbow or to the problem of doubling the square, how do we know what to do to make our situation intelligible to us? How does the work itself instruct us to see it, to move around within it?

One answer is the kind of work with a single, overall effect meant to be taken in and assessed as a whole. We glance at it, allotting to it no more than the time to have its first, or overall effect, an effect that takes half a minute or so. Such works do not require a passage through the details. With detailed works we need to ask just how the aesthetic effects are stored in the work, unlocked or played out in a long series of acts of attention and surprise. How do we find a run of sequences, of details, of small events echoed or completed somewhere else, the preparatory effects that announce a topic, the twists and turns of the unfolding of that topic, the climactic or ironic moments that bring it to a peak, the new statements or versions of it in another register? How do we know where a matter is announced, where we go to find its next steps, and variations, and how do we know when it has been discarded or brought to a satisfying resolution? These questions imply that just as with a proof or an explanation, we have to make a history or a narrative within our aesthetic experience, reduce it to steps and runs of steps. Like any all-at-once visual experience, the narrative arises out of the free play of attention that is unique to each viewer and to each occasion of resting for a time in the presence of the work.

But, is this narrative really an example of free play, willfulness, and the viewer's idiosyncrasy, or does it, as the example of the rainbow tried to show, result from a solicitation to attention built into the work itself that we might think of as an instruction to see this, to attend to just these details and, in the end, to discover just this or just that? The fact that we look at this and not that with thoughtful and fruitful curiosity is one of the most important features of the Cartesian or Socratic theory of wonder. Our attention and our pleasure engage us with just those things at the border of the unusual that we notice because we have the means to make progress with them. A civilization of geometry finds itself struck by the rainbow exactly because it possesses the means to think further about it, think part way along a path into it.

With a work of art we should expect to discover the same solicitation by just and only those objects that will in part reward time, curiosity, and exploration. The meaning of phrases like "struck by," "taken by," "attracted to," "fascinated by," in art no less than in science, suggests that here also we find a horizon of the unknown but knowable, a realm in which frustration and defeat are not the expected outcome. Any such narrative would be an account over time of our passage through the work, a narrative of how we found a question with its answer, a gesture with a response, a remark and its echo.

SEVEN

Thinking through the Work of Art

I will now look at two works, the first a work of singular impact, a work of one rich idea, a work, we might say, without parts, Cy Twombly's gigantic 1970 *Untitled*. The second will be a work that seems at first to have nothing but small-scale events, seemingly challenging us to organize them into narratives, into sequences, into questions and answers. Each of these two kinds of aesthetic challenge will have features in common with the poetics of thought that I have described for the rainbow and for the doubling of the square. These two works of art invite us, no less than the scientific examples, into the process of intelligibility, the path from wonder, surprise, a feeling of newness and attention-seizing freshness to curiosity, prolonged attention, satisfaction.

Cy Twombly's "Blackboard" Painting

We often find that the art of our own time, instead of renouncing the act of recognition, has redirected it away from the tradition, the stock of art and genres of art that make up our past, and toward the immediate surrounding culture itself, which can, in the work of art, be alluded to, mentioned, mocked, celebrated, or even transfigured.

These varieties of reference and recognition lead back to the familiar, but we find them now directed toward some shared memory from our everyday experience, not our knowledge of the history of art. Instead of a conversation with the tradition, we find a kind of intertextuality with everyday life.

We might call this painting of Twombly's a realistic work, even a trompe l'oeil work, because it seems to create ambiguity about whether it is a painting of a blackboard or, in fact, a real blackboard, covered with real chalk, hoisted up in front of us, sealed and exhibited as a painting. In Twombly's enormous, 13-by-21-feet blackboard painting the path of recognition that might lead us back to Rubens's or to David's mural-sized works is thin and relatively uninteresting, but the obvious variation on all that we know or have already experienced in our everyday lives about blackboards and writing, about schoolrooms and science, about how a blackboard is used and what size it ordinarily is, why it is so easy to erase, what kind of talking and writing goes on with a blackboard—all of these details of our everyday knowledge form the ground on which we recognize not just the gross fact that this painting is something like a representation of, or even an imitation of, a blackboard, but just why each and every detail that we are led to think about within the work is the way it is, resembling our experience, encouraging us to recognize, but establishing a rich play of differences from our ordinary experience. To look at the work we have to think out the collision of two recognitions: what a painting is and what writing on a blackboard with chalk is. By opening gaps or unexpected features within these two recognitions the work directs us, after our initial surprise and wonder, to a controlled set of questions and details. We begin from, I want to repeat, a classic state of wonder. We have never seen anything like this before. Its scale, simplicity, and loveliness, the elegance of the looping lines, its colorless beauty, strike us all at once. Its every detail is present for our first glance when we come across the work for the first time in a museum.

Twombly's painting solicits a very precise and ordered attention, now to this, now to that, and it gives us a very clear path to intelligibility. Each stage of our path to intelligibility depends on the back-and-

Figure 7.1 Twombly, *Untitled* (13 feet by 21 feet), 1970.

forth play between these two recognitions: this is a large, even monumental painting—and we know and feel many things about that; and this is a chalk-marked blackboard—and we know and feel many things in this case as well. An interference pattern is set off between the pair of recognitions, along with their details, that opens up the path to intelligibility.

Blackboards and Temporary Writing

A chalk-covered blackboard could be called the most temporary form of writing in our culture, a system made for easy erasure and reuse, but in a painting we have the most permanent form of an unalterable surface that we are to preserve just as it is forever. That is what our culture means by a painting, by a work of art. A blackboard is the very essence of a "blank slate." In Twombly's painting this most transient of forms (chalk on a blackboard) has been made eternal in a work of art. As art, it is an unerasable blackboard that will never be altered or opened up to other writing. That is the first difference between a blackboard and this painting of a blackboard.

As we stand and use a blackboard we commonly think out loud, and we do so, typically, in a classroom, a place of instruction and science. It is among mathematicians and physicists that a blackboard is an essential office or classroom tool. A painting that calls up blackboards sets itself into a pedagogic space, one where ongoing tentative thinking or exposition is usually found. But now the act of painting has frozen whatever inscription we see before our eyes.

The modest scale of an ordinary classroom slate reflects our need to reach any point on it from a standing position. This modest size Twombly's gigantic canvas has amplified. He has broken scale and monumentalized a comfortable, everyday piece of equipment. What giant could have a blackboard of this size? An ordinary blackboard is an aid, a secondary channel of information during a lecture. It is in the words of whoever stands at the blackboard that the major route to clarity occurs. No one stands near this blackboard. Silence rather than the teacher's voice accompanies the already complete writing. A blackboard is not intelligible without the teacher standing nearby, talking, writing, and periodically erasing. If we come into a classroom after a class is over, we often find that words have been left on the blackboard. They are now mysterious traces, dates and formulas, marks no longer in use, a kind of junkyard of writing. We erase it at once to be able to use it for our own notes. A filled-in blackboard is usually erased at once so that we can go on because writing and speaking need to move in parallel. If the board is filled, then there is naturally silence, just as there is in the empty classroom where we find the left-over words or formulas from an earlier class. Speaking, writing, and erasing are linked activities whenever the blackboard is fulfilling its function in ordinary life.

A blackboard is also always incomplete, never covered. In Twombly's painting the entire surface has been perfected, brought to a finish. What is, in everyday life, casual, smudged, messy, and accidental has taken on, in the painting, the orchestration of large-scale elegance and order.

However, the deepest surprise of the painting is not the monumental size, this heroic scale, this atmosphere of celebration, this eternalizing of the short-lived, but rather the puzzle that just where we would ordinarily find writing—that is, words, notes, formulas, diagrams, and problems—we find no words at all, no thoughts, no formulas or notes, but something like the abstract form of writing, the Platonic idea of writing that lies underneath all actual writing, or more simply, the muscular activity of writing without any goal other than that activity itself.

Ordinarily we would read a blackboard; here we must look. We must see, and in seeing, experience the deprivation of reading, of words, of sentences, of thoughts. But it is not absence that we experience, not loss, but rather the beauty of writing once words have been cleared away. We find instead an indecipherable and, for that reason, relaxing, unreadable writing. The move from reading to seeing has been accomplished. The sensuality of looping lines appears for our notice just where we would ordinarily be reading something, studying a formula. We do not miss the words; we do not even miss the fact of language. Just as much recent art has taken advantage of seeing to make us read, and often to read slogans, Twombly has promoted a culture of readers to the higher pleasure of seeing that takes place where reading used to be.

We are used to seeing words, even whole sentences, in contemporary art. When we find writing in art it often comes as something of a relief. *These* strokes I do recognize—they make up the word BLUE. They are easily construed, and we see how to set the questions that open up at least this part of the content. They also show us something about the scale of content in the work. Words rather than paragraphs, a word of this size, just so much of the canvas. And the word has been treated in one way or another—painted, drawn, stenciled, painted over, rendered incomplete, and so on.

In abstract art, iconic recognition weakened—there were no rocks and stones and trees, no men and women, no landscapes, no tables set with apples and no battles or crucifixions. Yet suddenly we began to see writing, almost as a concession or an anchoring bolt for the start of intelligibility. Now we find paintings filled with sentences, slogans, imperatives, paragraphs—bumper sticker paintings, propaganda, poster art—THE ENEMY IS ALWAYS WATCHING.

The writing that we find in the work of Jasper Johns or Twombly was an important provision of recognitions in a form that was mostly taking recognitions away. Cubism was the best early twentieth-century example of words turning up to allow "reading" just where object recognition, iconic and iconological recognition was being withdrawn or made more difficult. The glut of reading in the art of the past ten years—how many works turn out to be all words—stands for the same reassurance, but now in the face of an even deeper insecurity about the enterprise of art. Reading is always easier than seeing. In Twombly's blackboard the opposite occurs: instead of reading that is meant to help us out when we are having trouble giving coherence to seeing, seeing has been inserted just where we would expect the comforts of reading.

The promotion to the monumental scale of something homey and everyday, remembered from everyone's childhood schoolroom; the Platonic version of writing without words; the making eternal of a form of inscription usually washed clean every night or erased again and again even in an hour—all of these features encourage us to see a mysticism at work, a mysterious wilderness outside the village of the ordinary and the everyday. Of a size to be God's blackboard, although God never erases *His* thoughts, these lovely waving lines, layer over layer, become an image of thought itself, along with thought's play of variation, but adapted to an underlying sameness everywhere. Small differences of detail draw us on from place to place. The edges of the painting, enormous as it is, cut off an activity that we can see goes on beyond the frame, infinitely so far as we can tell, or forever. These 273 square feet, enormous as they are, seem like a few square yards of the Pacific Ocean or of the Milky Way. The frame gives us only a sample of an unendable activity.

We are meant in this painting to feel the relation of the everyday to the infinite, of the humble blackboard to a philosophical and monumental version of itself. Our memories of our childhood schoolroom learning are set in relation to the kind of seeing and to the kind of knowledge found in art. A very traditional heroic ideal of painting has been built out of everyday life's most casual surface.

If we start from the other direction—from the side of painting—we have to admit that Twombly's blackboard lacks many aspects of a traditional canvas, just as, from the other direction, the painting could be said to lack writing, words, the act of reading. This gray and chalky work is drab, lacking the color, form, texture, and imagery that we expect in a painting. It has a ghostly melancholy about it. If it is a Platonic blackboard, it is the minimal remains of a painting—like the mound of gray ash in a fireplace in relation to the logs or the living tree. These lines are not exactly drawing, just as chalk is not paint or ink. We notice that this looping skein of white overlays itself, creating layer after layer of depth. A lovely space has opened up because of these unerased layers of looping white lines over the neutral smudge of white. Because an ordinary blackboard is erased so regularly, it is part of its nature that we lose again and again whatever traces were on the board five minutes ago, yesterday, or last year. We do not create depth or the memory of prior states with a blackboard. The prior history of earlier lines does not remain (as they do here) fainter in the distance. The three-dimensional implied space of painting has been constructed out of exactly those materials—chalk, blackboard, erasure—designed never to create such space. The blackboard, a flat, pure present (the past has always been erased), has been made to appear in public with its past visible in the underlayers of scribble. Time has been brought into existence.

The canvas seems to contain an array of lines like a written page—twelve or so lines from the top to the bottom of the canvas. With these looping lines we see a mind that is neat, concentrated, recorded in both its abstraction and in its full intensity. It is obsessive and repetitive. Triviality and grandeur are indistinguishable from each other. The mind and the hand seem unstoppable, like the ongoing never-ending stream of interior thoughts or the flow of sensations; but in the painting they seem inconclusive, like murmuring rather than talking, humming rather than singing. Here we see what language would be like if there were no words, or thinking if there were no thoughts. This is what painting would have been like if there hadn't been any world.

The process of overwriting, smudging out, erasing, building layer over layer representing time, sequence, and the history of the motions of the hand that drew these graceful loops can go on for only a time. In space it could extend forever to the right and to the left, beyond the top and bottom of the canvas that we have here, but in depth, the layer upon layer would mean that soon it would be all white, all filled in, as uninteresting as the darker gray slate with which the process started. Only the middle point of this overwriting, this accumulation of layers, has this extraordinary vitality in which events that make a history some layers deep have been brought into being, but short of the point where too much experience has taken place and we see only white.

In a museum many viewers think they are seeing here a real blackboard marked with chalk, smudges, and erasures. Twombly's canvas painstakingly simulates the look of a blackboard. We see a near replication of the humble, everyday blackboard, a thing in itself easy to know directly. Why would we want this roundabout simulation of a blackboard, or is it here in front of us to pun on realism, on representation, on illusion and deception? Is this another version of Andy Warhol's Campbells Soup Can? Has abstract painting here turned back on itself to produce a new realism, a copy of the everyday world which turns out in its turn to be abstract?

In this work, which I found (perhaps from my horizon as a teacher) a stunning experience of wonder when I first saw it, we have the simplest case of "recognition" in contemporary art, and I have, in this brief description of it, called up the ordinary world off of which it works by resemblance, extension, contradiction, differentiation, change of scale, paradox, and monumentalization, by notation of feature, memory, and play of aspect.

If we were to think of this work as a work of American art in the generation after Jackson Pollock we could have taken a different, intertextual path, and situated its chalk and pedagogy, its cool, color-less skein of melancholy thought, in resemblance to and difference from Pollock's exuberant works. We could have recognized Pollock as the source insofar as his contrasting, mural-sized work would have let us think out Twombly's canvas. I did not do this because I wanted to stress the primary and very democratic recognition on which this work is founded. Twombly's painting does not depend on our creating a Clement Greenberg type of history into which it neatly fits: use of line after Pollock. The work is keyed to a much simpler, democratic act of recognition, what I would call lateral recognition, each person's memory of how a blackboard works in a schoolroom. It is this feature that makes this a work of a single overall impact, one situated within the poetics of recognition and variation, but now with the ordinary world of the viewer's life experience rather than the history of art or culture as its nexus of effects.

Such a work of art depends upon a single, overall impact, almost an idea, although to describe the idea without seeing the overwhelming scale and profundity of the work does not convey its force. The work has no parts or sections, no areas or segments. It does not call atten-tion to subcanvases—smaller wholes within the work. One syntax links any and every local stroke to the whole. There is, depending on your point of view, a daring economy of means or a poverty of means, of relations among areas, of scales as we pass from the smallest detail to the effect of the whole. In many ways the painting seeks effects like the music of Philip Glass or the theatrical work of Robert Wilson.

What can we see but one string looping, crossing, turning, changing direction, traces remaining from earlier layers, smudged areas like the Milky Way seen with the naked eye? So simple a means can be part either of the bourgeois aesthetic of boredom or of the saint's mysticism of oneness. The work constitutes a kind of universe both in scale and in simplicity. As Heraclitus said, all is fire; or Thales, all is water; this almost pre-Socratic work proclaims: all is writing.

In this painting we have a new version of the traditional theme of how the eternal power of art works in the face of the brevity and transience of life. The permanence of art has been arranged in an unexpected place within our own culture. This eternal blackboard contains a scene of erasable writing; it brings out the features of an impermanent medium meant for the moment, meant to be washed and reused, washed clean every night, meant to face us as a blank slate ready for our use. Here we find the traditional theme of Keats, Shakespeare, Horace, and of Greek art, the lastingness of art in spite of or even because of its subject, a transience that Keats called "fast-fading violets covered up with leaves." In Twombly's work we find a new version in a contemporary American idiom (blackboard and chalk) of the oldest theme in art, the basic point of many of Shakespeare's sonnets or Keats's odes. We also find repositioned the traditional pairing of fragility and monumentality, the delicate and the severely grand. Why in culture do we make just this or just that monumental? For what is this homage reserved? What is an inappropriate object for monumentality? What becomes merely inflated rather than monumental when we see it enlarged? Can the monumental coexist with delicacy?

Master Metaphors and Bright Ideas

The intelligibility of the mysterious and striking blackboard depended on the work being taken as a whole, as an idea. We set up a conversation between two familiar realms, the many things that we know and think about a painting and the many things that we know and think about the experience of a blackboard. The blackboard is being proposed as a surprising instance or location where we remember or recognize a package of traditional themes within art, such as these questions of duration, monumentality, illusionistic depth, the paradox of real-mimetic representation, and so on.

Like the water surface Monet used in this way or the tabletop used by Cézanne, or, more centrally, the window or mirror so familiar in earlier painting, the blackboard becomes one way to bring up again the deep questions of what kind of surface the surface of a painting is, what kind of relation to the real it suggests: is it a window onto the world outside itself, a mirror reflecting back, an agitated gel-like water surface, a tabletop where hand and eye assemble or compose already finished things, a bulletin board to which things are pinned in casual relation, a blackboard where the hand traces thoughts of the moment in the schoolroom of the world?

The pleasure of looking and thinking through such a fundamental work as this should remind us of a basic problem. A metaphor works only once. The first Twombly painting of this kind that we see raises fully all of these questions. Why would he paint more than one? We need to ask if this image could possibly be as fruitful as the tabletop of Cézanne, the watery surface of the late Monet, the window or mirror of earlier art, or is it what we might call a mere idea? What is left over for us if we enter a museum with ten or twelve works executed with this same premise? The poverty of grand ideas is just this suspicion of a kind of material poverty. Ideally, the artist would choose only the single best of these works and destroy all the others as preliminary versions of this one achieved masterpiece. Instead we are as likely to find ourselves thinking out this problem face to face with a minor variation of this genre in which the spell of presence in the work is far weaker than with the extraordinary one that we have looked at here. Or moving quickly in a Twombly retrospective, from one work to the next one, we find works too similar in kind to hold off boredom in exactly that situation where we began by being so taken with the freshness of the idea and the wonderful strangeness of the work.

Each of the master metaphors for art begins like Aristotle's pairing of echoes and rainbows as a cognitive sensation, an intellectual thrill. It unbinds the ordinary to return it to us remade: echoes and rainbows, blackboards and paintings. The border between fancy and imagination, between the clever and the profound, is harder to establish without the evidence of fruitfulness over time. Mirror, window, and tabletop are three master tropes for the surface of art. To propose another is always possible. Is Twombly's monumental blackboard a profound and fruitful master-trope or a quirky and quickly tedious bright idea?

The Work of Art as a Field of Details

When we begin from a kind of strangeness that does not yield at once the saving act of recognition, the prolongation of Cartesian wonder and its yield to curiosity are more readily traced. With Twombly's painting *Il Parnasso* of 1964 we find ourselves with a work that at first can seem nothing but details, casual in the way that scribbles are (Figure 7.2). Hard to take in as a whole at first, the canvas, wherever we look, captures us with small-scale events. This messy array of diverse details deliberately refuses to give anything to viewers who want a quick visual take. It demands immersion and a patience willing to invest time in looking at it, or nothing at all. The basic unit of the surface is a little free-standing burst of energy, a slight trace, a local and complete pulse. We see a line, a dab of paint, a splash, a splatter, a scribble, a scratch, a mark. Each is a kind of gesture and each gesture is in essence a thrill, a vibration, a shudder or rapid pulse. These are records of energy, vital bursts, a mimesis of pleasure. The canvas is a wide space for exquisite sensations, each given room to occur. We see free space separating one event from another. In time, these effects seem mimetic of pleasures that last only a few seconds, more like frissons, shivers, a thrill or ripple of muscular sensation, a first sip of unexpectedly cold wine, a shooting star, a gesture of great delicacy seen across a room, a brief smile. The painting makes short, impulsive traces that are as brief in space as these events are in time. They depict a realm of events lower in scale than the brief or transient things that Keats or Shakespeare thought transient—a flower, spring, a beautiful youth whose perfection five or ten years will take away. Twombly's events are almost too quick for the eye or for the memory. They are not anticipated or prepared for. They erupt unexpectedly and fade

Figure 7.2 Twombly's
Il Parnasso (81 inches by 86 inches), 1964.

quickly—a surge of pleasure like the entry of the flute in a symphony, or the first bite into an unexpectedly perfect summer peach. They are part of a sensuality beneath, below, too slight for what we call "experiences." They are part of the nervous life of surprises that is exhausting if too common, as the extraordinary orange color on the left of the painting would be if there were too much of it. These effects are not like a fully formed Mozart melody, but like a passing chord, a splice within sensations.

One deep question that such events raise is exactly the question of the limits of the tiny event. How small can a detail be and still be sensuous? Does the sensuous require a kind of languorous space in which to exist, does it require a time to savor? Is the minute at war with the sensuous, becoming more like irritation than pleasure? How small can a trace of color be and still be voluptuous? Certain colors within this painting are like the ripe-rococo colors of Fragonard or de Kooning, but now miniaturized. Sensuality does require a certain scale. The tiny is not sensual. In the other direction, a detail in order to be exquisite cannot be large.

These bursts of color, energy, line, and action are the starting point of the work. What syntax links them together? How does the work teach us to read it? A painting of this kind is made up of a set of subcanvases, units of intelligibility, smaller fields of action that propose familiar relations among parts, sequences, unfolding actions, and a final act of closure. I want to start with a clearly isolated episode or drama that occurs across the top of the work, like a sentence read from left to right (Figure 7.3).

A simple chalklike line enters from the left, white, underlined in faint blue. In its second stage it thickens as though made by a rapid back-and-forth stroke. Underneath it is a lovely closed form, a line reaching back across itself, a gentle, curving, pacific line, like a figure asleep. In the third stage, we see an agitated combat of white against black, green, blue, even a tiny speck of peach. Here the white line is animated into energetic play, a burst of spirals, as it stands face to face with elements and colors from elsewhere in the canvas. In a struggle of light and dark, a mating dance of female and male halves, the white is now brought to a pitch of energy in an antagonistic encounter with

Figure 7.3 Detail from *Il Parnasso,* left to right top strip.

things not itself, and it is subordinated to a larger closed form; both forms are inward looking, self-coiled scribbles of action.

This larger event near the mid-point of our passage across the canvas is the climax of a drama that began with the rather banal entrance of the horizontal, unassuming white line at the left edge. Now we have reached its vital, but highly civilized climax, where it is balled into a self-engaged patch, an area, a figural relation of two distinct halves, one dominant, the other defensive.

Last of all we have the aftermath, a thin ellipse, once again horizontal as the two stages before the climax had been. This loop looks back to the second stage but now makes clear the difference between preparing for the unleashing of energy and the very different state of resting in the aftermath of engagement. Now less lively and inventive than the relaxed looping figure of the second stage, it is slack, free of the drama of the climax.

These four stages create a narrative. We pass from a starting point, move on to development, then to a climax, and, finally, to a calm in repose—all passion spent. The white line is the stringlike element that we follow from left to right like an actor entering a scene. If the line still exists farther on at the far right it is only as a detail within a very misty area where white occurs as a minor element.

The action I have traced here and that, I think, Twombly isolates for us at the top of his canvas as a kind of simple training moment in the reading of the much more complex drama of the whole, this action is one of the subcanvases of the painting. It is a unit of syntax—the relations between individual words that endow them with a unifying sense. On this scale, intelligibility first occurs. The subcanvas stands apart because a drawing-like, four-stage action using one color unfolds and ends within a local sector of the canvas.

The episode is unified by its drawing technique, by the simplicity of its elements, and by the placement of the four stages in a row from left to right. The color white, the elegant drawing hand at work, the buildup and release of energy, and the play between self-relation (coiling) and encounter with another element (combat or engagement) make up the economy of means.

The climactic stage of this sequence, in the upper center of the work, larger than the rest, is a dancelike pair of figures that we see many analogs for elsewhere in the painting (Figure 7.4).

Figure 7.4   Detail from *Il Parnasso*, the key episode of Figure 7.3.

The coupled, figural forms which we find everywhere in the painting, always in the same scale, lead us to a key set of subcanvases. They mark out, we might say, the size of the unit of sense. In language a letter is not a unit of sense. Sometimes a word (five or six letters on the average), sometimes a phrase (two to six words long), a sentence, or a paragraph defines a unit of sense, the smallest location of intelligibility.

With the explanations of the rainbow it turned out that the unit of intelligibility was the raindrop and the pair of rainbows. For the doubled square it was an artifact—the larger square in which the starting point and ending point, problem and solution were incorporated as parts—that was needed before intelligibility was possible.

If we return to the larger canvas we can see that the system of white drawing in this subcanvas was part of a linked arc of white that shapes the painting. We can go on to trace this larger intelligible unit. Starting from the vertical lines at the lower left, we rise to the sudden flower of white under the black scribble at the top, to the subcanvas already described, to the crossing variations of white underneath it, arriving climactically at the white, full, painted (not drawn) figural partner of the brown dancelike character on the right. This pair constitutes one of the greatest subcanvases of the painting, the one central to its vitality, one of the canvas's most striking dancelike couples (Figure 7.5).

Figure 7.5   Detail from *Il Parnasso*, middle right.

In this figural pair, with its left-side white actor, the color white reaches what we might call personhood, or personlike reality. Within the painting, a sequence never ends with such a near-human mark with its feeling of energy, bodily intelligence, and upright position. Instead the use of white leads us on as it continues down to the white traces that end at the bottom right with the fence of white writing that tilts and falls away with a flowerlike tiny reminder of white beneath it that touches the lower edge. This fence or scribble of white has a partner opposite (at the top left) in the scribble of black. These opposite corners form a kind of pairing that is very different from the face-to-face couples that give greatest energy to the painting. To trace this large intelligible unit of white, scaling in its arc across the entire canvas, is to accept the training of the small episode we began with, taking it is a primer for how to work with the materials of the painting, how to find syntax.

We might ask what it is in the painting itself that suggests we think of it as made up of subcanvases that we turn to in our attempt to read it. Is it only that every work of art must be made up of parts that draw our attention? Is there a stronger case to be made here, a claim that the painting itself is instructing us in how to look at it with prolonged attention?

Several features of *Il Parnasso* suggest that this is the case. First, to any eye this is a painting made up of areas where certain colors are used that are absent elsewhere. Each of these colors defines a domain or a narrative of which it is the central actor. Second, the painting is also made up of differentiated techniques of drawing, painting, washes of paint, raw lumps of paint, and many variations. These in turn define ordered domains: drawing, scribbling, writing, painting,

Figure 7.6 Detail from *Il Parnasso,* lower left.

veil-like washes. Third, and more explicitly, we can see near the bottom that a set of rectangular lines on the left implies that this area—roughly one twelfth of the whole—be, for a time, regarded as complete, as a composition, as a painting within the painting outlined for our attention by a frame of lines (Figure 7.6).

The lines and edge of the canvas shelter our attention, point out just how much of the space should be regarded as a unit of intelligibility. Within this arena, we find one of the most beautiful, sensuous pairings of two energetic figures, one black and the other a luscious pink orange figure, both musical, agitated, alive with erotic energy and with mirroring excitement. The two seem to stimulate each other into exuberance, the highest aliveness of color or paint (Figure 7.7).

Figure 7.7   Detail from *Il Parnasso,* the central actors from Figure 7.6.

Across the canvas, another set of drawn rectangular lines along with the cluster of red and crimson defines a further subcanvas, leading us to the obvious fact that we always look for answering subcanvases across the central space of the work (Figure 7.8).

In combination, these three aspects tell us to group by area in order to create intelligibility. We dwell for a time now in this, now in that subcanvas of the painting.

Once we have worked through the pairings of nearby, face-to-face "figures" and the echoic, more distant contrasted pairs opposite each other along one or another axis of symmetry, we can see, given enough time and pleasure in the individual episodes, that this local order is the start of a rich syntax in the work. It is the work's "geometry." Our attention is drawn to events or patches of a certain scale. Should we next try to trace each effect that we find on this scale in

Figure 7.8   Detail from *Il Parnasso,* lower right.

smaller and smaller details, or does it operate just at this one scale within the work? For example, these side-by-side or face-to-face couples, always in two distinct colors, but unified by technique such as the skeins of thin lines in the white and black drawn pair at the top, or worked paint brushed into shape as in the orange and black pair on the left—are they repeated in the tiny spots or pairs of dabs one tenth the size of these paired figures?

Here we need to pause to question the kind of vocabulary that I have been using. Does every act of seemingly naive description smuggle recognitions back in without admitting it? Why call certain areas of paint, but only some and not others, "figural" and then speak of pairs of such shapes as couples? Are we making them male and female, and is this really to be seen as a dance, or as Eros or even as mating? Haven't I recognized, as we tend to do in the twentieth century, that all stories in the end boil down to sexual stories? Haven't I fallen back on the familiar, readymade recognitions of our culture and historical moment? Sexual patterns, energy interpreted as struggle or combat, things occurring in twos as couples? Why isolate the space around each possible pair rather than study only individual shapes except that doing so will allow us to call it a couple, a sexual mating, a dance of male and female? For our culture these micro-scripts are covert recognitions, easy to hand. Were we fifteenth-century citizens of Florence we might have found many "virgins with child" wherever we saw one large, one small shape; we might have isolated every possible grouping of three and talked of trinity relations. We could have seen feudal protection, and the gradation of orders and places in society. One feature of recognition is that even when we try not to depend on it we still use a hazy repertoire of all-purpose stories that draw scratches, dabs, and points of information together.

What is it that gives legitimacy to any language of persons and relationships here where we see only dabs and blobs of paint? And why a sexual vocabulary? Should we now go on to divide all colors in the painting into masculine and feminine, making our division an occasion to smuggle in the standing clichés of our culture about masculine power, darkness, aggression, larger size, and so on, versus feminine softness, lightness, delicacy, defensiveness, receptivity?

These words of caution are needed because although all descriptive language uses passing references and recognitions that work as what we call suggestions, we need to restrict the power of these suggestions by varying them, letting loose more and more varied currents of implication so that description does not relax into the worst possible version of recognition, in which any set of traces or marks can be allegorized into our favorite narrative of the moment, whether that is the narrative of the sexual, the narrative of the material and the spiritual, the narrative of fall and redemption, the narrative of struggle, or any one of the other skeleton keys that seem to open every door, but only because such doors in fact weren't locked in the first place.

It seems to me essential that no one say, "Oh, I see that I didn't get it before, but now I see that it's all sexual" or "it's all" anything else. The feeling "I get it!" or "It all comes down to X" is the idea of intelligibility that I am working against and working to present an alternative to.

To return to these double shapes, we should ask whether there is only a scattered array of these paired figures or whether they, like the narrative at the top of the canvas, unfold toward a dramatic climax of intensity. The ultimate subcanvas of this kind is the white, brown, and black set of figures on the right, just above the red and crimson open play of circular and bloblike forms (Figure 7.9).

Figure 7.9   Detail from *Il Parnasso,* three figures.

Here, the subdued drama of three mysteriously individuated shapes gives a more sober, more veiled version of the pair of black and peach figures on the left, the youthful, voluptuous pairing across from the more contained triangle of actors.

Once we move back to a larger scale we see that the many subcanvases looked at so far are locked into larger dramas of which they in turn are only phases. The right section of the canvas is such a unit. It ascends from bottom to top as a kind of history of paint, of matter, from crude blobs of sculptural material to figural drama to veiled, gauzy aftermath, a climax at the top right of extraordinary refinement, delicacy, and memory (Figure 7.10).

Or at the other side of the painting, if we begin near the bottom on the left we find three smudges of orange-peach paint, thick matter rising off the canvas in simple shapes, mere dabs or splotches. They seem *unworked,* unbrushed or unshaped, pure matter without human

Figure 7.10 Detail from
Il Parnasso, right side.

use. We could think of them as matter not yet infused with either labor or thought. Rising above these dabs we have streaks of orange in a triplet that has been thinned-out and shaped as small rising wisps. Above them we find the largest use of the color, rich in shape, layered with pink and traces of green and brown and facing a wilder, rich black figure in a dancelike relation. The orange-peach figure has written above it the name of the Greek poet Sappho. This event, the Sappho figure, is the peak of engagement, of size, and of importance, the figural climax of the progression (Figure 7.11).

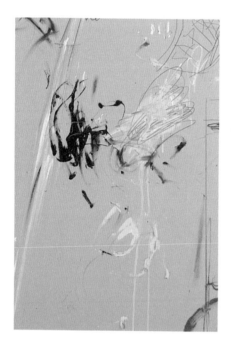

Figure 7.11   Detail from *Il Parnasso,* peach series with the figure of Sappho.

· ·

Above and to the right, the same peach color enters as a mystical thin veil within the central white figure of the canvas. As an under-painted highlight under green, under white just below the figure, the color turns into a waterlike trail, in serpentines of white and pink. Tiny specks of the same color occur above and to the right. What has driven this progression from thick small spots of unfigured paint to brushed, to figural, to veils and traces? The color has no presence on the right side of the painting at all. On that side vermilion and crimson replace it, mirroring its spiritualized effects in a declamatory, ripened style, high summer to its delicate spring. In the clever upper center of the canvas the orange and pink colors play out their slight, final, delicate effects as a counterpoint to white.

As we look at the range of demonstrated technique, we can see Twombly's self-consciousness and pleasure in exploring side-by-side paint without painting (mere paint) alongside painting, color, washes of color, drawing, writing, scribbling, and other material subjects. We can see that the canvas sets up a scale that begins with pure color impasto, paint as we would find it on the palette, squeezed from tubes, mere stuff, usually in single, free-standing colors, and usually in the lower third of the canvas, where earth gives weight to landscapes. We see on the left the dabs of peach, on the right a mud of brown, black, or crimson in raised sculptural thickness.

But as the eye rises into the air of the painting, the paint becomes thin, veil-like, active or line-like. It flies, turns, and blends with other colors. It is overpainted, layered, rich in relations, less like matter. At the upper right of the canvas a smeary air of colors and looping lines, blue-green and white, one of the most poetic and lovely of subcanvases, gives the atmospheric climax of the work (Figure 7.12).

Figure 7.12 Detail from *Il Parnasso,* upper right.

Here we find a place where all definiteness, all figural individuality—elevated as that individuality or figure-like shape might seem in relation to the crude matter below it—is now dissolved into a spiritual final state. Rising from base to top, we pass from primal claylike stuff, to figural being, to the encounter of figures with others in couples that are sometimes erotic or combative, sometimes dancelike partners that are fused or even mated, to mysterious higher-level blended spiritual configurations purged of both Eros and strife. The sky of the painting belongs to the gods.

The central subcanvas, which would take as long again to discuss as all that we have done so far, is a small-scale, refined, watery world of white and orange, of writing, words, and numbers lacking the force and pressure of the events to the right and to the left, but turned down to exquisite effects of elegance and delight. This is the part labeled "Apollo," where effects that we are used to from the bold colors and larger shapes at the right and left have now been made exquisite (Figure 7.13).

Figure 7.13   Detail from *Il Parnasso*, Apollo.

By engaging with the details of this apparently casual work, a work that includes so many scribbles that some would describe it as scribbled or graffiti-like (a terrible mistake, in my opinion), I have tried to show that just as with the rainbow, the doubled square, or the black-board painting, the initial strangeness, the unplaceable quality of the work, yields to the same curiosity as the more clearly problem-like cases of wonder that we have earlier considered. We are led on by captured attention, drawn on by pleasure, instructed to solve or group what can, within our horizon of knowledge, still occur as the know-able, the resolvable. When we look at a work like Twombly's *Il Parnasso* we are clearly outside the ordinary, facing the strange and the as yet unhistoricized. While the process that I have gone through briefly puts us on several paths to what is knowable within the painting, they do not in any way let us say: "Now I get it!" We do not face a puzzle here that will have a sudden answer. Instead we are in front of a work that invites prolonged attention, partial satisfaction, the play of hypotheses and sequences. Intelligibility is partial, more like the feeling, after a period of time, of what we call knowing our way around the work, as we know our way around a city.

The Return of Recognition and Memory

Although I have claimed that intelligibility for this work has to be built up from a script built into the work itself, a syntax has to be found that links the details into features and narratives, dramas in some cases. Although this has been my naive procedure here, I now have to admit that an entirely different process would have been possible, one based exactly on the source hunting of traditional art criticism, and therefore on memory and recognition.

The painting has its title written within it "Il Parnasso." We also see the artist's name, Cy Twombly, the place and date, Roma, 1964. If we look for other words we see Sappho, Apollo, Dante, and a set of numbers across the center, 4, 5, 6, 7, 8, 9. Vaguely we also see the 1, 2, and 3, each above sets of strokes that march across the upper center. In fact, the center of the canvas is where most writing occurs, along with scratches through lines that we use to cross out writing that we want to cancel. The name "Dante," for example, is scratched out in just this familiar way, not erased or removed but present in cancellation. For some, these words, along with the title, will suggest that

Twombly's painting is, in fact, a version of, a variation on, or (informal as it is) a set of notes on Raphael's Stanza fresco, *Parnassus,* in the Vatican. Poussin had earlier produced a version of Raphael's work, certainly one of the most famous works in our tradition (Figure 7.14).

Once we have compared the two works, we might feel that we are helpless without the Raphael as a source. The painting represents Apollo, the nine muses, the mountain Parnassus, and a number of recognizable writers, the blind Homer, Dante, Sappho with her name just above her head exactly as it is above the orange, pink figure in Twombly's painting. It seems, in fact, that intelligibility in this case is no more difficult than looking back and forth between the Raphael and the Twombly to explain every feature of the second in terms of its variation or use of the first. The odd shape of the missing center is now clearly the opening in the wall that Raphael had to work around. The rounded feeling of the action at the center of the Twombly refers to the actual shape of Raphael's wall.

Recognition seems to give us much to do. Match this to that, this bit over here is a version of that, and so on. But what do we know if we know all of this? We know a lot of strange information that does not give us the very sense of the Twombly work, its sensuality or its syntax, its issues, its play between drawing, writing, painting, and the mudlike matter of paint as raw material.

We seem to know. With recognitions we suddenly regard the work as a coded translation, like a Morse code version of a Shakespeare sonnet. Once we replace the dots and dashes with letters, words, and the fourteen lines of verse, we are back on comfortable territory. Why should this seem to dispel the unfamiliarity of the work, its strangeness? If we search Raphael's painting for its topics and syntax we will have, I think, a set of matters entirely different from those that Twombly uses this strange resemblance to bring up. The two paintings are about two altogether different things. And the process by which we might come to know our way around one or the other is distinct. The Raphael gives us no clues at all to getting to know the Twombly painting, no clues to what I have been calling intelligibility. By contrast, within Twombly's canvas there is, as I have shown, a built-in primer in the strip of events that runs from left to right across the top

Figure 7.14 Raphael, *Parnassus.*

of the work that teaches us to read the larger more complex work and to enjoy its episodes and syntax.

In short, by bringing up the alternative of recognition, situating Twombly's painting within a tradition of precedent works, we actually come to know little about the work, unless we then set off to investigate the very features with which I naively began, features to which we are drawn by the pleasure and energy of materials set up within the work itself. The Raphael source functions more like the biblical story of the rainbow; it sets the details to rest and wraps the sensuous experience, the attraction of pleasure, into an overall distracting explanation.

Once we know Twombly's painting on its own terms, and Raphael's fresco on its terms, the link between the two is, in itself, of real interest. Following Poussin and Raphael, Cy Twombly celebrates art, and, more important, the technical, physical mystery of his own art, painting, by means of a tribute to the rival art of poetry with its great masters Homer, Sappho, and Dante, whose names appear on the canvas in script alongside his own signature. Named for the hill of the muses in Greek mythology, *Parnassus* is both a monumental canvas and a page of writing. One subject of the painting is how extremes of scale like the monumental and the apparently tiny and casual can be set in relation. The written words on the canvas maintain their everyday size or scale as words on an ordinary page while as gestures they link up into a monumental canvas each of whose elements is local in space like the few stars in the night sky. All art begins in matter and in humble material. How do we get from humble scribbles to poetry or even to the name Sappho? Do we dare to write the name with such casual quick gestures? How does the gross, bloblike matter of paint become the ethereal spiritualized matter of art?

One paradox of this work is based on the power of the minute. Intense, local scribbles or patches of color with only a nearby field of action (much like a small face in a large canvas) are linked in pairs, often with partner areas far away in the field of the work. Local series of sets of marks, runs of color and binary pairs, build a larger syntax for the self-contained, energetic gesture-like details. Paint in all its material forms, from crudest, thick matter to etherealized haze or thin, blended spiritualized trace, is used to give a landscape-like modulation from earth to ground to air to sky. The figure marked Apollo near the upper center is a climax of spiritualized matter, an exquisite trace of the high-energy action of art.

In his abstract idiom, Twombly sets out to find the capacity within his vocabulary to bring about the same effects of locally bundled features, self-contained and powerful within however large a work, that realistic artists had available in any tiny area recognized and attended to as a face. At the same time he attempts to deliver the overall organization of matter and spirit, earth and air, bottom and top, weight and lightness that made up the realists' large-scale, point-to-point organization called a landscape.

Finally, Twombly sets out to show here that the idiom of abstract art is itself the spiritualization, the etherealization of earlier realistic idioms, preserving the combination of local intensity, which in writing is a word, or in realism a face, with the complex ordered wholeness that is, in writing, a poem made up of those words, and in the traditional painting of Poussin and Raphael a monumental landscape depicting the paradise of art which each artist, in the act of painting it, claims to join by taking his place among the names in paradise: Sappho, Homer, Dante, Twombly.

· · · · · · · ·

The process of intelligibility that I have illustrated through my examples is, I think, the answer to questions or doubts about proceeding at all, doubts about giving sustained attention to the work. In Cartesian vocabulary, the strangeness or newness is here combined with visual pleasure and with the intimation of an order and a purpose. Accepting the path of sensuality and the steps from pleasure to pleasure— those of color, shape, scale, order—we find our way not to a moment of solving the painting, but to knowing it. We mean by that, being acquainted with it, seeing part of the intelligibility of it as Aristotle, Theodoric, Descartes, or Newton saw part of the intelligibility of the rainbow. The idea, in either case, of an explanation that dispels wonder or curiosity is the wrong model to carry into the situation, with the rainbow and the doubled square no less than the Twombly painting. The magnet, which in the Renaissance was always the second most prominent instance of wonder along with the rainbow, was, in the great work of Gilbert, not explained away. We know more about it if we read his book, and today we know even more or different things about it, but anyone, even an adult watching the horseshoe magnet seize a nail or drive away another magnet, is still in the situation that I have tried to describe as central to intelligibility, a situation involving not answered questions, dispelled wonder, but rather a horizon between the familiar and uninteresting, too pointless for thought and pleasure, and on the other side the unknowable or unthinkable, equally uninteresting for thought because it is subject only to kinds of thinking unanchored to detail or test. In that middle zone the poetics of wonder occurs.

Notes · Acknowledgments · Index

Notes

1 The Aesthetics of Rare Experiences

1. T. E. Hulme, *Speculations: Essays on Humanism and the Philosophy of Art,* ed. Herbert Read (London: K. Paul, Trench, Trubner & Co., 1924).
2. Plato, *Theaetetus,* trans. Harold North Fowler (Cambridge: Harvard University Press, 1952), 155c, p. 55.
3. Ibid., 155d, p. 55.
4. Ludwig Wittgenstein, *The Blue and Brown Books* (New York: Harper & Row, 1965), pp. 127–130.
5. T. S. Eliot, *Four Quartets* (New York: Harcourt, Brace & World, 1943), p. 15.
6. William Shakespeare, *Cymbeline,* 4.2.262–263.
7. Vladimir Nabokov, *The Gift* (New York: Vintage Books, 1991), p. 6.
8. Ibid., p. 29.
9. Dante, *Paradiso,* trans. Allen Mandelbaum (New York: Bantam, 1986), Canto 2, ll. 97–105.
10. Michel Authier, "La réfraction et 'l'oubli' cartésien," in Michel Serres, ed., *Eléments d'histoire des sciences* (Paris: Bordas, 1989), p. 251.

2 The Rainbow and Cartesian Wonder

1. Ralph Waldo Emerson, *The Collected Works,* ed. Robert E. Spiller and Alfred R. Ferguson (Cambridge: Harvard University Press, 1971), vol. 1, pp. 8–9.

2. Carl B. Boyer, *The Rainbow: From Myth to Mathematics* (Princeton: Princeton University Press, 1987), p. 53.

3. Quoted in A. C. Crombie, *Robert Grosseteste and the Origins of Experimental Science, 1100–1700* (Oxford: Clarendon Press, 1953), p. 159.

4. Plato, *Theaetetus,* trans. Harold North Fowler (Cambridge: Harvard University Press, 1952), 155c, p. 55.

5. René Descartes, letter of February 22, 1638, in *Oeuvres philosophiques* (Paris: Garnier, 1967), vol. 2, p. 25.

6. Ibid., vol. 1, p. 719.

7. Ibid., vol. 1, p. 651

8. Ibid., vol. 1, p. 749.

9. Ibid., vol. 3, pp. 1006, 1009–1010.

10. David Hume, *A Treatise of Human Nature* (Baltimore: Penguin, 1969), 2.9 pp. 492–494.

11. Blaise Pascal, *Pensées,* trans. A. J. Krailsheimer (Baltimore: Penguin, 1966), p. 95.

12. Ibid., pp. 89–90.

13. René Descartes, *The Philosophical Works of Descartes,* trans. Elizabeth S. Haldane and G. R. T. Ross (Cambridge: Cambridge University Press, 1986), vol. 1, p. 411.

14. Pascal, "Le mémorial," in *Pensées,* p. 310.

15. Descartes, *The Philosophical Works,* vol. 1, pp. 365–366.

3 Wonder and the Steps of Thought

1. Aristotle, "Metaphysics," trans. W. D. Ross, in Richard McKeon, ed., *Introduction to Aristotle* (New York: Modern Library, 1947), 1.980a, vol. 1, p. 243.

2. Ernst Mach, *The Science of Mechanics: A Critical and Historical Account of Its Development,* trans. Thomas J. McCormack (Lasalle, Ill.: Open Court, 1960), pp. 40–41.

3. René Descartes, *The Philosophical Works of Descartes,* trans. Elizabeth S. Haldane and G. R. T. Ross (Cambridge: Cambridge University Press, 1986), vol. 1, p. 69.

4. Albert O. Hirschman, *The Passions and the Interests: Political Arguments for Capitalism before Its Triumph* (Princeton: Princeton University Press, 1977).

5. A. C. Crombie, *Robert Grosseteste and the Origins of Experimental Science, 1100–1700* (Oxford: Clarendon Press, 1953), p. 277.

4 Explanation and the Aesthetics of the Rainbow

1. William Wordsworth, *Selected Poems and Prefaces,* ed. Jack Stillinger (Boston: Houghton Mifflin, 1965), p. 160.
2. John Keats, *Complete Poems,* ed. Jack Stillinger (Cambridge: Harvard University Press, 1982), p. 357.
3. Carl B. Boyer, *The Rainbow: From Myth to Mathematics* (Princeton: Princeton University Press, 1987), pp. 28–29.
4. Quoted in A. C. Crombie, *Robert Grosseteste and the Origins of Experimental Science, 1100–1700* (Oxford: Clarendon Press, 1953), pp. 156–157.
5. Ibid., p. 244, emphasis added.
6. Ibid., p. 244.
7. Isaac Newton, *Opticks* (New York: Dover, 1979), book 1, part 2, proposition 9, problem 4, pp. 174–175. Emphasis added.
8. René Descartes, *Les météores,* in *Discours de la méthode* (Paris: Fayard, 1987), p. 303.
9. Boyer, *Rainbow,* p. 203.
10. Ibid., pp. 211–212.
11. Ibid., p. 315.

5 Transition to Aesthetic Wonder

1. René Descartes, *Oeuvres philosophiques* (Paris: Garnier, 1967), vol. 1, p. 87.
2. Ibid., vol. 1, p. 87.
3. Ibid., vol. 1, p. 186.
4. Ibid., vol. 1, p. 189.
5. Blaise Pascal, *Pensées,* trans. A. J. Krailsheimer (Baltimore: Penguin, 1966), p. 225.

6 Intelligibility, Wonder, and Recognition

1. Roland Barthes, *The Pleasure of the Text,* trans. Richard Miller (New York: Hill and Wang, 1975), pp. 39–40.

Acknowledgments

An early version of this book profited from the intellectual vitality and scholarly support of the Wissenschaftskolleg zu Berlin (Institute for Advanced Study, Berlin). An invitation to deliver the Una Lectures at the Townsend Center for the Humanities at the University of California, Berkeley, allowed me to present a version of the argument of this book and to profit from the responses of many friends and colleagues at Berkeley. A version of part of Chapters 3 and 4 was presented as a lecture at the Institute for Advanced Study, Princeton, and I am grateful to Princeton University Press for the right to reprint those parts of my lecture later included in the volume commemorating Irwin Panofsky. Both James Cuno and Ivan Gaskell of the Harvard University Art Museums offered valuable comments on the final manuscript.

For the right to reproduce works of art and photographs I wish to thank the following:

Figure 7.1. Cy Twombly. *Untitled,* 1970. House paint and crayon on canvas, 13 feet 3 and $\frac{3}{8}$ inches by 21 feet and $\frac{1}{8}$ inch (405 × 640.3 centimeters). The Museum of Modern Art, New York. Acquired through the Lillie P. Bliss Bequest (by exchange). Photograph © 1998 The Museum of Modern Art, New York.

Figure 7.2. Cy Twombly, *Il Parnasso,* 1964. Oil and graphite on canvas, 81 by 86 inches. Collection of Mr. and Mrs. Graham Gund. Photograph: Greg Heins. I am grateful to the artist, Cy Twombly, for his permission to reproduce his work.

Figure 7.14. Raphael, *Parnassus.* Photograph: Vatican Museums.

Index